unstuck at last

unstuck at last

USING YOUR STRENGTHS
TO GET WHAT YOU WANT

SARAH K. ROBINSON

ISBN-13: 978-0-9861073-0-6

www.FreshConceptsOnline.com

To David, Dawson, Jack, and Hope with all my love

And in loving memory of Carole Robinson, a woman who knew the key to being unstuck was pushing forward, being positive, and loving fiercely.

Contents

Introduction.. xi

Chapter 1: Feeling Stuck.. 1

    What are your wildest dreams?.. 4

    Exercise: Dream BIG 7

Chapter 2: Tapping Into Your Uniqueness 9

    What makes you unique?.. 11

    What are your Strengths?.. 11

    What are your motivators? 15

    What are your values? 17

    What is your vision? 21

    Feeling Inspired?... 23

    Exercise: Your Unique Self... 29

Chaper 3: Who's That in the Mirror? 31

    Getting in the Arena 35

    What's Your Story?... 38

    Exercise: Create a Positive Story Playlist 40

Chapter 4: Change Ahead 43

Using Your Strengths to Accept Change 45
Exercise: Strength-Based Change 49

Chapter 5: 20/20 Vision 51

Self-Discovery Brings Clarity to Your World 53
When Strengths are Underappreciated 56
Downsides? 58
Exercise: Assessing Your Progress 59

Chapter 6: Frenemies and Champions 61

Frenemy Defined 64
Champion Defined 65
Breaking Free 66
Exercise: Discovering Champions 68

Chapter 7: Lead by Recognizing the Strengths of Others 71

Accept the "Daily Thanks" Challenge 74
Exercise: Becoming a Strengths Leader & Champion .78

Chapter 8: Perspective Is Everything 79

Blind Spot 80
Productive Partnerships 81
In the Wrong Place 83
Perspective Abuse 84
Exercise: Yin and Yang Together at Last 86

Chapter 9: Get Gritty 89

How Gritty Are You? 90
Grit and Goals 91
Gritty Interviews 92
Gritty Movie Characters and Historical Figures 93
Getting Gritty with Your Strengths 94
Exercise: Gritty Insights 97

Chapter 10: Amelioration - Continuous Improvement ... 99

    Ameliorate at Any Age...100
    Continual Improvement Is Not a New Idea 101

Notes & Citations 107
Acknowledgments 113
About the Author 115

Introduction

This book is written for anyone who knows the feeling of being stuck – cemented in place by gravity, inertia, or some other-worldly force – and is seeking liberation.

This is your one life. Why settle for anything less than being your best every day and achieving your greatest dreams? My goal in writing this book is to create a personalized map that allows you to **get stronger and stronger** every day. I promise it will be an exciting journey filled with moments of greater self-understanding and fulfillment.

There have been countless books written to help individuals find their path and realize their dreams. I've read many of them. And I've enjoyed and learned so much about myself by being open to the advice of others. Sadly, I never found a book that focused on my particular characteristics and helped me to harness my unique qualities to get exactly what I wanted out of life. Deep down I knew I was capable of more than I was accomplishing personally and professionally. I felt both stuck and like the world's heaviest monkey was strapped on my back, insisting he would not get off until I found my calling, my path, my reason for being. It's been said that you write what you know, and feeling stuck is something I know about.

I was quietly but painfully stuck for twenty-some years. It's hard to admit. Even my closest friends were not aware of how desperately stuck I felt. The trouble with being stuck is that you see no way out. I was sure that the wretched feelings I had about myself, my life, and my unrealized goals would never lift. I had entered a stuck life-sentence without parole. There were no doors or windows that hinted at a possible escape route.

By most people's measure, I did not appear obviously stuck. In fact, for more than 20 years I served as a consultant to organizations that wanted to become unstuck. I helped them listen to their employees' needs by applying feedback tools like employee satisfaction surveys, team-based questionnaires, and focus groups. Frequently an analysis of employees' feedback would reveal organizational dysfunctions that were subsequently addressed through group training or one-on-one coaching sessions.

Unfortunately, I still had that dreaded feeling that this was not what I was supposed to be doing. In 2002, I took on a teaching role with the vague hope that this might resolve some of my angst. It wasn't a total fix, but being a college instructor has led to some wonderful growth both personally and professionally.

As a college instructor, I have helped thousands of students learn the fundamentals of organizational behavior. Essentially, I teach my students what makes a manager great, a team productive, a leader critical, and an organization successful. My hope is that my students – armed with this knowledge – are able to steer their future organizations away from dysfunction and toward organizational health.

For about 10 years, I balanced my time between teaching and consulting. Once the challenge of the joint roles wore off, that sinking feeling resumed. In 2011, I decided I needed to broaden my organizational behavior expertise. In 2013, I was among the first seven individuals worldwide to become a Gallup Certified Strengths Coach. Since that time, I have devoted my consulting practice entirely to individual and corporate Strengths coaching.

As a Strengths coach, I use my unique skills every day. But more importantly, I help other people to use their Strengths daily. Deciding to focus all my energies and attention on what I do best was an intentional, but difficult, choice. The world encourages us to focus on our weaknesses and compensate for them. Whose parents didn't send the message that they were more worried about the "C" than the "A"? At work, we shroud our deficiencies, hoping no one will notice what we are lacking. But spending our energies in this way is self-defeating. We spend so much time spinning our wheels on activities that are not naturally suited to our talents that there is little time left to delve into our favorite areas of interest that – importantly – reveal our Strengths. It is in these favorite areas where we have the greatest chance for success.

Before, when I was stuck, I tried to be the best consultant or instructor I could be. Inevitably, this meant imitating others who I thought were good consultants or instructors. Now, I try to use my unique Strengths to be the best ME that I can be while in the roles of consultant or instructor. This switch in focus has led to a watershed change in me. I am unstuck at last.

Today, given my personal journey to become unstuck and my professional experience helping people and the businesses they work for become great, I feel more prepared than ever to share the ups and downs of my journey and the journeys of those who have traveled a similar route.

Sometimes my clients are professionally fulfilled but personally stuck, while other times they are content at home but feel stymied in the workplace. Regardless of the location of their roadblock, I have come to see that coaching lifts the veil that has been over them, allowing them to see themselves and the world more clearly.

As I've stated, I'm a Gallup Certified Strengths Coach. Within these pages, I have shared my coaching toolbox. For this reason – and due to the profound impact that knowing my Strengths has had upon becoming personally unstuck and helping others to become unstuck – **I'm asking you to learn and appreciate your Strengths by taking the Clifton StrengthsFinder® Assessment.** The words in this book will be hollow and devoid of real meaning until you understand your own Strengths.

How do you do that? It's very easy. You need to join the ranks of millions that know their Strengths by devoting 35-45 minutes to taking an online assessment. You can go to **www.unstuckatlast.com/resources** to be directed to the Gallup homepage where you can take the assessment for about the cost of a lunch.

In order to take full advantage of the tools I have in store for you, you'll also need to actively participate and engage yourself in the reading of this book. There are exercises – usually consisting of multiple steps - at the end of each chapter. These exercises are intended to pry you lose, push you forward, and propel you into your bright future.

Learning occurs more rapidly when we are active, not passive. Who hasn't felt like dozing off in the middle of a lecture? This book should not be anything like a lecture. The dozing occurs because we are being passive, sitting in our chairs trying to absorb information that may or may not be relevant to us. Contrast this passive learning to the learning that occurs in a science lab or interactive workshop. The activities that occur in the lab or workshop keep you from dozing, and ignite your learning. This is because you're active, not passive, in the learning process.

The exercises at the end of each chapter are meant to be completed prior to moving on to the next chapter because they will actively engage you. Passively reading each chapter, without actively engaging in the exercises, will be as futile as watching an exercise video without doing the workout: possibly entertaining, but not likely to improve your fitness.

Spoiler alert:

Chapter two includes four mid-chapter exercises that I've entitled "Do It Now". It's really important that you do these exercises before starting Chapter three. Of greatest importance is taking the Clifton StrengthsFinder® assessment. *Unstuck At Last* is a guide for people who want to use their Strengths to become unstuck. While I present a number of other tools and assessments that are helpful in your journey to become unstuck, your "Top 5 Strengths," as discussed in your Clifton StrengthsFinder® results, will be referenced again and again in this book.

As to the amount of time you should allocate to the process of becoming unstuck, I leave that up to you. If you have a bee in your bonnet and feel the immediate need to immerse yourself in the process of becoming unstuck, you could read this book and compete all of the exercises over a weekend. Most people will need a few weeks to digest this information and evaluate how it pertains to them personally. If you read a chapter each week, and both contemplate and fully complete the exercises at the end of each chapter, it will take 10 weeks to both read and actively participate in the learning outlined in this book.

Being stuck can feel like the first 12-hours of a 24-hour virus. In those first hours of sickness, it is difficult to have faith that you will get better as your symptoms are becoming more pronounced. You may momentarily convince yourself that you will never be free of the full-body aches, fever, and lethargy that have overtaken your normally healthy body. Similarly, being stuck can make you believe that you will never be fulfilled and shouldn't even aspire to be fulfilled. Why try? But, just like a virus, once you get through those first 12 hours, you can and will get better. These pages contain the antidote to your ills.

Ready to start?

one

Feeling Stuck

Most of my adult life has been spent feeling stuck. And while feeling stuck is disconcerting, it is that sinking feeling that "there is something else I'm supposed to be doing" that has pushed me forward and forced me to seek answers in the most unsuspected places. I've been frantically looking for things that would squash that nagging internal voice of discontent since 1998.

Initially, I thought my feelings of being stuck were due to my inability to conceive a third child. I was positive that three was our number. I have two siblings and my husband is one of five. My beautiful, healthy, and sometimes wild and crazy boys did not seem like enough family and chaos.

The boys were five and three years-old in 1998. Like most young boys, they wanted a pet. Every outing where we encountered an animal (anytime we left the house) was a chance to remind me of that fact. I responded to their frequent requests for a puppy by telling them that "we will get a dog when the next baby is out of diapers." The baby I was referring to was not yet conceived despite months upon months of Clomid®, temperature taking, and good old-fashioned try-ing.

For those who are happily oblivious to the term Clomid, it is a drug that can help men and women to conceive. When taken by women, it sets in play a series of hormonal changes that ultimately stimulate the ovaries and boost ovulation. For the individuals for whom this drug works, it's a lifesaver. For those who use it and are unsuccessful, it is a nightmare. Clomid side effects can include mood swings, hot flashes, bloating, abdominal pain, headache, and general crabbiness with the world.

The most difficult side effect I experienced was the monthly cycle of raised hopes and crushing disappointment. Despite my efforts to trick my body into ovulating, the ulti-mate goal of conception would not happen. My friends con-tinued to conceive at remarkable speed. It was salt to my open wound. I uttered words of congratulations to my happy friends while I silently lamented my lack of success.

In 1999, I had an epiphany. I realized that I needed to get off the dime (and the Clomid) and move things along in a more productive direction. After three years of monthly re-minders confirming my failure to obtain the one thing I knew I needed (a third baby), I felt bruised and weary. Despite my private desperation and increasing irrationality, I had a tiny sliver of sanity left. The rational piece of me knew I was be-ing unreasonable. I felt guilty that I had two amazing children but did not feel done. I realized how lucky I was on so many levels, and decided that I needed to let my dream for a third baby go. It was a sad relief to concede and quit trying to ac-complish something that was clearly so out of my reach. I had to move on.

We got a chocolate Labrador retriever for Christmas 1999. He was my brown haired and brown-eyed furry baby. He looked just like me. I loved him as did his brothers and his dad. He was my third baby boy and we named him Wellfleet, Fleet for short.

I decided to go back to school. I already had a master's degree in Industrial and Organizational Psychology and a fledgling business that focused on satisfaction surveys and training, but I was not feeling inspired and excited by my work. I decided to jump into an area about which I had little knowledge but lots of interest: theology.

In mid-January 2000, just after the holidays settled down and before my theology classes started, my husband and I went out to celebrate a new year and a new beginning for me. We had had a great New Year's Eve celebration with friends, but this night was for us . . . and by that I mean me. We toasted my exciting plans to go back to school and had a fantastic dinner. Three weeks later I realized I was pregnant with our third child.

My sister-in-law, Lee, is that one who remarked a few months after Hope's birth that my third baby, and only girl, completed me. And Lee was right, kind of. Hope's birth renewed my personal belief that things do work out if you keep pressing along. When one door closes, another opens. You just have to keep at it and take a different tack. Sometimes giving up completely is the exact tack that makes sense. But that only works as long as you start something else, and that means continuing to look for ways to grow and expand your horizons.

Ok, I realize that my baby Hope story is cliché. Possibly it sounds like every "when we finally gave up, that's when it happened!" story you've ever heard. But I tell it for two reasons. First, it explains how that very difficult period in my life led to a great deal of learning.

It set a paradigm in place that is a large theme in this book: if it doesn't feel right, it probably isn't. More importantly, the status quo is not going to fix it.

Second, if that thing you thought made you incomplete gets resolved and you still feel incomplete, you were just wrong the first time. You've got to keep trying to move forward. A sense of resolution will come, if, and only if, you can hang in there. I promise.

What are your wildest dreams?

"Our creative dreams and yearnings come from some divine source. As we move toward our dreams, we move toward our divinity."

- Julia Cameron, *The Artist's Way*[1]

During this next period of my life, which I'll call "I feel so much better, but still not complete," I realized that my inability to conceive a third baby was not the source of my feeling stuck, nor was a master's in Theology going to complete me. Don't get me wrong – having a baby girl was a wild dream come true. But she did not fill the hole that was inside me. Similarly, going back to school was thoroughly enjoyable and intellectually invigorating. Although I lasted only a few semesters in the program, it was a crucial step for me developmentally. I reconnected with my love for writing and recognized how much I missed the academic world. Soon after I exited the Theology program, I was asked if I wanted to teach a college course related to organizational behavior. I jumped at the chance. Importantly, I might not have leapt so quickly or with as much enthusiasm without this short stint at the local seminary.

During this time, as I came to recognize that a third child and subsequent graduate degree were not the right fixes, I was continuing to search for antidotes to my feelings of being stuck. Although, I did not consider myself an artist, I felt stuck in the way that artists discuss being creatively stuck. I read Julia Cameron's book *The Artist's Way*[1] and was drawn to her insights about creativity. Although the advice within her book related to becoming artistically unstuck, her words thoroughly resonated with me.

I came to believe that we all are born creative beings and that we lose that creativity along the way to adulthood due to limiting beliefs, fear, self-sabotage, and guilt. Reading *The Artist's Way* allowed me to pinpoint the exact moment I disengaged creatively. I had lost my belief in my artistic self at a specific moment in eighth grade.

Although I had had some artistic success in grade school, I remember getting the artistic rug pulled out from under me in middle school. I vividly recall working on a still-life assignment and being shocked at my ineptness. My artwork was terrible compared with that of my more artistic friends. I was embarrassed by my lack of ability and, despite my early success in grade-school art competitions, I decided that I lacked talent and that art classes were a waste of my time. I quit.

Mind you, I had not received a scathing review of my art that shook me to the core. I made this decision based on my limiting beliefs and my judgment that my work was inferior. At that time, I assumed that artistic talent was God-given, not something that was cultivated and grown with hard work and determination. I had what is referred to as a fixed mindset about creative talent. I believed that some people have it and some people don't. And there isn't much to do if you don't have it but move on.

Stanford University psychologist Carol Dweck strongly refutes the notion of a fixed mindset and counters it with a revolutionary alternative – the growth mindset. She explains that those people (like my eighth grade self) who believe that talent is God-given are opposed to effort and challenge. Sadly, Dweck's research shows that the fixed mindset has negative repercussions of many kinds for the individuals who hold it, including preventing those individuals from setting difficult challenges for themselves[3].

The growth mindset group believes that learning and being smart is about setting difficult challenges, even if those challenges bring failure. Furthermore, the growth mindset proponents believe that smart people learn from failure. This thinking is diametrically opposed to the ideas of the fixed mindset individuals who believe failure only confirms an individual's lack of talent or smarts.

Our wildest dreams can be severely limited by having a fixed mindset. Why dream big if your core belief is that you lack the talent to obtain those dreams? **My world changed when I switched from a fixed mindset to a growth mindset.** I'm not sure exactly when this switch occurred, possibly reading Cameron's wisdom about creativity being a growth process opened my eyes to the fact that everything is a growth process. Who knows? All I know for sure is that my new growth mindset made many things possible that I once considered impossible.

Stella Terrill Mann said, "Desire, ask, believe, receive."[4] Recognizing that I felt stuck allowed me to tap into my deepest desires. I desired something more. I was awakening to the idea that something was missing. I had to ask myself time and time again "What is it that I really really want from this one life I am living?" Only when I was able to believe that my dreams were possible was I ready to receive.

Today, I am able to honestly say I am doing EX-ACTLY what I'm meant to do. It is like the world's heaviest monkey has been lifted off my back. I want that for you.

Exercise: Dream BIG

What are your wildest dreams and desires for the future? Ask yourself,

"What great thing would I pursue and therefore achieve if I knew I could not fail?"

Robert Schuller's words "What great thing would you attempt if you knew you could not fail" are similar. I prefer "pursue and therefore achieve" because it hints at the goal of this exercise: to set your sights on an achievement. The sky is the limit.

Consider three lives that you could live and write a complete story of what that each life looks like. Make these fantasy lives wildly different from one another. You can base these lives on people you know (or know of), or they can be original compilations of the kind of life you want to live. Each dream should include as many details about your fantasy life as possible.

Consider the following questions:

Where would you live geographically?
What type of home would you have?
What would your family look like?
What kind of people would you spend time with?
What kind of professional life would you have?
What type of achievements would you be most proud of?
Who would be your greatest supporters?

two

Tapping Into Your Uniqueness

Do you remember when you learned that your thumbprint was unique to you? I recall being both dumbfounded and intrigued by this remarkable new fact. Could it be that no one on the planet had a thumbprint just like mine? The lines on my friends' thumbs looked similar, if not identical, to mine. I wondered what made each of our thumbprints special, different, and distinct. Given my inability to see those differences first-hand, I reasoned that there were microscopic differences that only a trained eye could detect. There was comfort in knowing that my uniqueness – my specialness –could be confirmed by an expert of some kind.

Ideally, children are bolstered by teachers, preachers, parents, and loved ones who reassure them that they are special. But somewhere along the way to adulthood we stop hearing how special and unique we are. The world tells us we need to "get a real job," "stop dreaming," and "grow up." If we succumb to the pressure and believe these messages, we may even ridicule others who are still chasing their dreams.

Understanding what makes each of us unique in our professional and personal lives has considerably more personal value than contemplating the uniqueness of the lines on our thumbs. Surprisingly, it is more difficult for most people to distinguish our differences from others than it is to recognize our similarities. Our similarities are easy to spot and tie us to humanity. We quickly recognize that we have two arms, two legs, and one belly button and that these physical features match the anatomy of our friends and loved ones. It's a relief to know we belong. Conversely, our differences take more introspection or at least a broadened perspective. It is comparable to having a scrape on the tip of one's chin: easy for others to see and difficult for us to see on our own.

As a college instructor, I receive candid assessments from students at the end of each semester. I've taught the same course three times a year for over 10 years and received more than a thousand evaluations from my students. Depending on the grade they've received, they may not necessarily be objective, but their comments can shed light on my strengths and weaknesses in the classroom.

Without a doubt, the most prevalent theme in these written comments from students is their recognition of my enthusiasm for teaching. It took years of receiving variations of the same feedback ("freakishly enthusiastic about subject matter") to recognize that my natural excitement for and desire to discuss leadership, motivation, job satisfaction, and a host of other organizational behavior topics was a unique quality.

What makes you unique?

There is a freedom and a focus that comes from fully acknowledging our uniqueness. Do you know your unique gifts and talents? Can you articulate them in a way that resonates with friends, employers, and the world?

Your uniqueness is built based on your Strengths, Motivators, Values and Vision. Understanding each of these layers helps you fully appreciate your unique gifts.

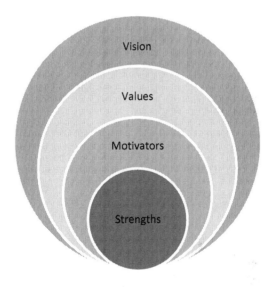

What are your Strengths?

Your Strengths are the core of who you are. Although you have had your Strengths all of your adult life, you may not have recognized how important they are to your success and happiness. When your Strengths are used to help you navigate your daily behaviors, career goals, and relationships, they will serve as the epicenter that gives your life focus and meaning.

Do It Now

1. Can you list your "Top 5 Strengths"? If you have not done so already, please take the Clifton StrengthsFinder® assessment and learn your unique gifts. Gallup, the corporation that owns the tool, predicts that 1 billion people will come to know their strengths in the coming years.

   Go to **www.unstuckatlast.com/resources** to take the assessment and learn your results, which are also referred to as your "Top 5 Signature Themes".

   These five themes, or Strengths, are unique to you. Only one person in 33 million will have your results, meaning the chances are very slim that you will ever meet another person with the same "Top 5 Strengths" in the exact same order as you have.

   The Clifton's StrengthsFinder® assessment is comprised of "34 Themes" which I will consistently refer to as Strengths throughout this book. A brief definition of each Strength is presented on the next two pages. The 2007 book *StrengthsFinder 2.0* by Tom Rath[1] is a great resource for those who are interested in gaining a more thorough understanding of all 34 Strengths. This list should NOT be used as a means to guestimate which Strengths apply best to you. There is no replacement for taking the assessment. It's mandatory.

   Similarly, these definitions only scratch the surface of explaining each of the 34 Strengths. The individualized report that is generated after you take the assessment will give you far greater insight into your Strengths.

Strengths:

Achiever®: a hard worker and list maker.

Activator®: an initiator and action-taker.

Adaptability®: an accommodating group member.

Analytical®: a logical decision maker.

Arranger®: an energetic multi-tasker.

Belief®: an ethical and self-sacrificing team player.

Command®: a conflict revealer.

Competition®: an always striving challenge-seeker.

Communication®: an expressive story-teller.

Connectedness®: a spiritual soul.

Consistency®: an equality enforcer.

Context®: a history buff and background checker.

Deliberative® – a cautious decision-maker.

Developer®– a people-potential recognizer.

Discipline® - an organized worker and tidy home-owner.

Empathy® - an understanding listener.

Focus® - a directed doer.

Futuristic® – a forecaster and prediction-giver.

Harmony®– an agreement seeker.

Ideation®– a creative solution giver.

Includer® – a welcoming and inclusive host.

Individualization® – a differences appreciator.

Input® – an information and thing collector.

Intellection® – a thoughtful ponderer.

Learner® – an interested student.

Maximizer® – an excellence seeker.

Positivity® – a cheerleader with a joyful spirit.

Relator® – an authentic friend.

Responsibility® – an oath keeper.

Restorative® – a problem solver.

Self-Assurance® – an independent influencer.

Significance® – a recognition chaser.

Strategic® – a big-picture planner.

Woo® – a diverse and dynamic connection maker

2. Do you have copies of past performance reviews or testimonials from customers, friends, or colleagues that you can re-read? Do you recall a recent compliment that made your day? Is there a theme that emerges when reviewing your professional and personal accomplishments? Are there connections between your "Top 5 Strengths" and these compliments?

3. What has been your biggest achievement in the last 12 months? Recall a personal or professional success that was especially rewarding to you. What happened? How did the success make you feel? Did your Strengths play a role in making that success happen? If so, how?

Recognizing your natural gifts and cultivating those gifts is your first step in becoming unstuck. Below is a diagram that explains how each of us is layered just as the center of the earth has layers or the trunk of a tree has rings.

What are your motivators?

Your motivators are the second layer radiating from your epicenter. Understanding what motivates you is critical to directing your strengths toward the correct activities. Occasionally I encounter individuals who claim that their strengths are not aligned with a job that they are excited to perform. They question me, "Why do I dread the idea of being a ____, when I have the skills to capably perform the job?"

First and foremost, your Strengths do not dictate the exact profession you should pursue. In fact, your Strengths can be used in a number of ways but really should not be used as a hiring tool. Second, what these individuals are experiencing is a lack of MOTIVATION to pursue a certain profession, even when they recognize that their natural talents and skills seem to make them "perfect" for the field.

For example, you could realize that you have strong Analytical skills and a gift with numbers but do not find the idea of a career in accounting even vaguely interesting. Or you could have a great passion for history and have a strong love of learning. Given these two facts, a college professor might seem a logical choice for a career. This path will lead to lack of fulfillment if a life of teaching and researching sounds like a jail term.

Your motivators, coupled with your Strengths, tell you what you WANT to do and what you do WELL. Understanding both your Strengths and your motivators can help you make decisions related to career choice, volunteer activities, fitness routines, or hobbies.

Some motivators ignite a sense of passion to work all night long because you love what you are doing, while other motivators are geared more toward completing work, because only then will you receive the recognition and external rewards that you desire. Psychologists refer to these two types of motivation as internal motivators and external motivators.

Do It Now

The list below contains both internal motivators and external motivators. **Choose the five motivators that are most important to you.** These do not need to be motivators that you currently experience at work or at home. Choose the motivators that would most inspire you to accomplish a task.

Motivators:

o Your ideas are supported and encouraged.

o Every day you are completing different tasks and are never bored.

o You have colleagues who remember to celebrate your work anniversary, birthday, and personal accomplishments.

o You are rewarded with money for your achievements.

o You are rewarded with recognition for your achievements.

o You are able to engage in win-lose competitions.

o You can take your pet to work with you.

o You have freedom over your work schedule.

o You are able to establish your own goals and create your own timeline to accomplish them.

o The person you respect most at work compliments you.

o You are encouraged to pursue educational opportunities and certifications related to your career path.

o You are encouraged to be creative.

o You are given a new title.

o You are able to establish and enforce a set process to streamline your work.

o You are recognized by your peers as a top performer or contributor.

o You are recognized by your boss as a top performer or contributor.

o You are able to balance your work and family obligations.

o You feel valued by the people you work with.

o Your company's CEO commends your performance.

o You have a close friend at work with whom you share personal and professional concerns and triumphs.

o You receive an all-expenses paid vacation.

o Add a motivator not listed here.

What are your values?

Hopefully, you now have a better understanding of your unique strengths and the things that really motivate you. The next layer to consider is an assessment of your values. Living a life that is true to your values is a critical part of living a complete and unstuck life. When we do things, say things, or spend our time in ways that are not consistent with our values, we have regret. It is a buyer's remorse type of feeling about how we've used our precious time here on earth. Our gut recognizes when we use our time in a way that does not line up with who we think we are or who we want to be. In a nutshell, regret overcomes us when our time is ill spent.

Logically, it follows that most of us try to avoid putting ourselves in positions where we feel regret. We associate regret with disappointment, unhappiness, grief, and heartbreak. In her book *The Top Five Regrets of Dying*, Bronnie ChaWare[2] gives us a peak into end of life regrets. Ware cared for patients in the final weeks of their lives and recorded their common regrets. Below is a list of these patients' most frequent concerns.

1. I wish I'd had the courage to live a life true to myself, not the life others expected of me.

2. I wish I didn't work so hard.

3. I wish I'd had the courage to express my feelings.

4. I wish I had stayed in touch with my friends.

5. I wish I had let myself be happier.

This is a great list to put in your pocket and take out every now and again to put your daily trials and tribulations into perspective. But what is at the heart of these regrets? I believe they stem from living a life that was unaligned with each person's values. I believe that living a life that isn't true to your core values could set all of these regrets in motion.

Being true to oneself and one's core values is a bit of a paradox, in that it seems like it should be as easy as falling off a log, yet it can be a lifelong struggle to achieve. From the psychological perspective, we may not be our true selves because we believe we need to act a certain way or say a particular thing to please our boss, spouse, or parents. This social pressure to act contrary to our true nature can be intense. If you are constantly trying to impress others or live up to the expectations of others, you are living an inauthentic life.

Living without authenticity can make you feel tired, anxious, confused, depressed, helpless, or angry. It can make you feel incomplete and stuck. Given these negative consequences, it's not a surprise that it tops the list of "End of Life Regrets."

Being authentic or "being true to oneself" means getting clear about the things that are important to you. It means that you must come to understand what you value and live a life that is consistent with those values. Research in the field of organizational behavior has found that authenticity is positively associated with well-being at work. Why? Because if you are able to live and work in a way that expresses your values and personal truths, that promotes well-being.

Keeping up appearances and always doing things that make others happy without considering your own happiness means you are sacrificing a piece of yourself. It makes sense that being authentic – or living your life in a way that is consistent with your values – is correlated with psychological well-being, including vitality, self-esteem, and coping skills.

Let's consider how likely it would be for a person who is living authentically to work too much, hide his feelings, lose touch with friends, or shun happiness. It seems unlikely, doesn't it? Living authentically and according to your values promotes listening to that voice inside yourself that encourages you to put limits on work, express your true feelings, stay connected with friends, and embrace happiness.

When your actions mirror your values, your daily regrets diminish and your personal satisfaction increases.

Do It Now

Assess the list of values below. Circle the **five** that are most important to you.

Appreciation of Beauty and Excellence

Bravery

Creativity

Curiosity

Fairness

Forgiveness

Gratitude

Honesty

Hope

Humility

Humor

Judgment

Kindness

Leadership

Love

Love of Learning

Perseverance

Perspective

Prudence

Self Regulation

Social Intelligence

Spirituality

Teamwork

If you are interested in assessing your values in a more objective fashion, take the free personality assessment, called the VIA Character Survey. VIA, the organization that owns the rights to this survey, refers to the results as being character strengths. I will refer to these results as values, not character strengths, to keep these results distinct from the Clifton StrengthsFinder® results which will be referred to as Strengths.

    Go to **www.unstuckatlast.com/resources** to be directed to the Values assessment.

What is your vision?

Thus far, we have explored how words can be used to describe your uniqueness. We have tried to discover what you do well, what motivates you to pursue a goal, and what values you bring to every situation you encounter. Choosing a vision that inspires you will engage a different – nonverbal – area of your brain and give you a new perspective on your abilities.

Do It Now

The next active learning exercise taps into your ability to visualize your uniqueness. I would like you to choose only ONE photograph that ties together your abilities, your motivation, and your values. Happily, it sounds more challenging than it really is.

    You will be asked to review 50 photos but you'll naturally gravitate toward a handful of them. You will need to be cutthroat and decisive when narrowing this group to five photos that inspire you. When looking at the website where the photographs are placed, ask yourself, "Does this remind me of me?" Once you have whittled the photos down to five winning photos, give each a more thorough analysis. Ask the following questions to find the single, BEST, photo.

1. Why does this remind me of me?

2. How are my abilities visually represented in this photo?

3. How does this photo relate to one or more of my motivators?

4. Are my values captured in this photo?

Go to the **www.unstuckatlast.com/resources** to review 50 black and white vision photos.

This photo of the sunrays fighting their way through the dark clouds is my favorite image because it is hopeful – my second most important value. It reminds me that, given my competitive nature, I want to beat the odds. This photo makes me feel both energized and calm at the same time. It inspires me to see the light when there is darkness all around. Ultimately, it is a beautiful photo that challenges me to be me.

You may not see any of those things when you look at this photo, and that is perfectly okay. After you choose your favorite photo, do not feel the need to get input on your analysis from others. It is irrelevant. Your vision is a tool solely for your own inspiration and imagination.

Feeling Inspired?

Contemplating your uniqueness - your strengths, your motivators, your vision, and your values – is inspiring, right? I hope doing so gives you the feeling of small butterflies growing in your stomach. Nervousness, anticipation, and uncertainty might be dominant emotions if you have been suppressing your true self and are beginning to recognize the power of your many gifts. On the flip side, living an unaware and restrained life can make you feel unfulfilled.

If the term *inspired* seems too lofty, think again. Without inspiration, life has less meaning, joy, frustration, heartbreak, excitement, and disappointment. If you hold the common misconception that inspiration is just for famous artists or struggling inventors, you are dead wrong. Being inspired is critical to being unstuck regardless of your station in life or career path. But this next phase of growth comes with a warning: being inspired may be uncomfortable. **If you are feeling a bit confused and uncertain as you consider your strengths and your values – a combination of ants-in-your-pants nervousness and dread – you are headed in the right direction.**

Most adults have a healthy aversion to the nervousness that inspiration can bring. Nervousness is a feeling that many people associate with embarrassment and failure. As children, we were frequently forced to push ourselves through nervousness and emerge on the other side of it. Whether the occasions that made us nervous as kids are related to public speaking, boy-girl interactions, or getting ready for that big exam, we rarely had the option of bowing out completely.

As adults, we have considerably more control over our lives, and we can use that control on ways that limit us. We are tempted to completely eliminate situations that prompt nervousness. We say things silently to ourselves and openly to others like "oh, I don't do public speaking," "we don't know each other; it would be uncomfortable for me to introduce myself," or "I can't sign-up for the certification, I'm not a test taker."

Avoiding all situations that prompt nervousness and the minor discomfort that goes with it is a bad idea.

I urge you to embrace a little bit of nervousness and even make friends with the butterflies in your stomach. Expect these butterflies to emerge on a regular basis. They are a sign that you are growing and challenging yourself to live an inspired and unstuck life. **Total terror is not what I am recommending.** In fact, I am supportive of staying far, far away from terrifying situations. What I am encouraging you to do is to honestly evaluate why some situations make you anxious. Possibly, these situations are opportunities for growth and fulfillment.

Below are a few examples of how your personal and professional lives can be enriched by overcoming those little butterflies that may be holding you back from some terrific experiences.

Challenge Yourself Physically: Whether you sign-up for a 5K race or want to tackle an Ironman, athletic challenges require you to harness your physical and mental energies. Virtually all athletes will tell you that their sport has required them to develop some level of mental toughness. But the example below shows that you do not need to consider yourself super athletic to gain from the benefits that athleticism can bring.

While working with Lisa, a successful real estate executive, she and I quickly recognized that her professional self was thriving but her personal life was floundering. After a bit of coaching it became clear that she needed to reintegrate her strengths into her non-working life. Over the last 20 years, she had her foot firmly on the "work" accelerator and had forgone developing her interests outside of work. Unfortunately, she was riding the brake when it came to using her strengths in her personal life.

Lisa's boss worried that she spent too many late nights and weekends at work, and he openly encouraged her to slow down at work and allow herself more freedom and downtime. He reminded her that she had a terrific staff. But she was hesitant to delegate. Despite having a fantastic support system in her boss and staff, she could not change her ways. She was stuck in a pattern of behavior that felt safe, albeit unhealthy and lopsided. Work continued to trump any and all other activities.

I asked Lisa about hobbies she might consider. She quickly responded that she had been a runner in the past, but gave it up. I asked her, "Why did you stop running?" She couldn't remember. What she did remember, and proudly shared, was that she had entered a number of 5K races when she was training and had improved her time at each subsequent race.

It was immediately apparent to both of us why these races were so fulfilling for her and why she needed to start running and racing again. Lisa has Competition in her Clifton StrengthsFinder® "Top 5 Strengths." Given this strength, Lisa loves win-lose competitions. She was pouring this strength into her days and nights of work but needed to ignite her Competition in her personal life in order to have balance.

Once she realized that her competitive spirit fueled her wherever she might be – at work, at home, at the fitness center – she understood how to channel it. Lisa came to realize that being competitive has many definitions. At work, Lisa used her Competition to win – straight up. At home, Lisa felt best about herself when she applied this same strength to a recreational activity. When Lisa harnessed her Competition to beat her last 5K race time, she knew she wasn't going to win the entire race or even her age bracket as a new runner, but she delighted in seeing her incremental improvements.

Lisa was racing against herself and found the same thrill from this type of competition as she did from her real estate wins at work.

Take a Social Risk: Are your social circles growing, at a standstill, or diminishing? Because of social-media tools, joining a group has never been easier. However, I am not advising you to check out Match.com or to grow your LinkedIn connections. I am encouraging you to affiliate yourself with individuals who are like-minded.

Has your new understanding of your Strengths and values revealed that you love intellectual discussions and value creativity? If so, take a look at social networking groups that organize discussions on the national, regional, or local level and make a plan to visit local art shows. Are you rediscovering your love of learning and your interest in foreign food and ethnic cultures? Challenge yourself to eat at a restaurant that is known for its authenticity. Talk to the owner or find recipes on-line, and invite friends over to enjoy your freshly created feast.

These are just a few examples of how **any combination of Strengths and values can be creatively combined to help you sniff out a new affinity group** that speaks to your uniqueness and inspires next steps to completeness. There is so much to gain and so little to lose from activities such as these.

Learn a Professional Skill: The thought of looking stupid at work makes most people cringe with embarrassment. Happily, there is an entire training industry geared toward helping professionals learn new skills while keeping embarrassment to a minimum.

Facebook's COO, Sheryl Sandberg, writes in her book *Lean In*[1], that early in her career a colleague was horrified to realize that Sandberg did not know the computer program Lotus 1-2-3. She feared being fired. Well, guess what. Even Harvard graduates don't know everything. Sandberg was not fired by her boss—he taught her Lotus 1-2-3 instead.

Challenge yourself to learn a skill that can be added to your professional resume. Public speaking classes, computer courses, and certifications in your field await you. **Exploring new professional opportunities is nerve-wracking but has many potential benefits . . . including better self-insight.**

Break Your Daily Habits – If Only Temporarily: Breaking out of your daily routine can feel uncomfortable but can also lead to inspiration. One way to quickly shake up your familiar pattern is to change your living situation. Be forewarned that swiftly changing your habitat can induce culture shock. Organizational behavior specialists use the term culture shock to explain the physical and psychological symptoms (like excessive hand washing or illogical fears) people experience after being abruptly placed in a new culture.

However, there are also many benefits that can be gleaned from a foreign culture. Immersing yourself in a world that is different from your own – wherever that culture may be: big city, small town, seaside village, or foreign destination – can enrich your understanding of how your current culture impacts your habits.

Breaking old habits and trying out new habits, such as testing whether you actually prefer tea to coffee in the morning, can open your eyes to a brand new and unfamiliar world. This new view of the world can help you see, use, and appreciate your Strengths.

Rene, my sister-in-law, spent seven months living in Nairobi, Kenya, hoping, praying, and waiting for news about the impending adoption of Eva, a beautiful 6-month-old she met while visiting Kenyan orphanages. During those days and nights away from her husband and three children in the United States, she had to embrace the life and culture around her or be consumed by doubt and uncertainty.

In Nairobi, Rene found unlimited opportunities to change her routine. Like most Americans, Rene took her car to get groceries and run errands. In Nairobi, Rene walked everywhere: to get food, check the status of her adoption paperwork, and bring water to her third-floor apartment. At first, her new routines seemed scary and unfamiliar, but over time they became more comfortable. She was living a real-life adventure that had an unknown ending.

The most challenging issue for Rene was her need for patience. She was – at heart – an impatient American, who like most Americans, felt entitled to having 24-hour stores around each corner and helpful, prompt service when needed. In sharp contrast, being patient was a way of life for most of Nairobi's citizens. When the water stopped working or the electricity was out, Rene found that questioning her neighbors, "What led to the outage and when might power be returned?" prompted blank stares. If she could be patient, her questions might be answered.

Rene relied on her Strengths of Activator and Positivity while in Nairobi. As an Activator, Rene relentlessly looked for new opportunities that might further the processing of her adoption paperwork. Her Positivity allowed her to hold on to her Belief that it would all work out. Given the almost insurmountable obstacles around her – obstacles the likes of which she would have never encountered in the U.S. – Rene's Strengths made it possible for her to persevere.

As we will discuss in more depth in Chapter 3 (Who's That in the Mirror?), Rene continued to tell herself the right story about how this adventure might end. She continued to believe that "if I fiercely pursue this dream of adopting Eva and put all of my positive energies into this task, the right thing will happen." She knew that "the right thing" might mean that Eva stayed in Nairobi.

It was a huge risk to put her life on hold and her heart on her sleeve in pursuit of Eva. But in the end, Rene and Tom were able to adopt Eva on April 6, 2005. After seven months of living away from the rest of her family, numerous tearful phone calls, and plenty of doubting moments, the right thing happened for Rene and Tom. **Our daily habits can make us feel comfortable and secure, but may also prevent us from exploring new ways of living and limit growth.**

Exercise: Your Unique Self

1. **Write the following four lists and post them somewhere where you will see them daily.** A form to record these has also been included in the back of this book.

List 1: Top Five Strengths

If you do not already know your results, take the Clifton StrengthsFinder® assessment to discover your Strengths. **www.unstuckatlast.com/resources**

List 2: Top Five Motivators

The list of motivators is presented on pages 16-17 under the 'Do It Now' heading.

List 3: Top Two Values

The list of values is presented on page 20 under the 'Do It Now' heading. The VIA Character Assessment can be found at **www.unstuckatlast.com/resources**

List 4: Inspiring Vision

There are 50 visions, of which you need to choose one, at **www.unstuckatlast.com/resources**.

2. **Journal Writing:** After contemplating the ideas presented in this chapter, identify **three** activities that might that ignite your strengths, motivators, values, and vision. Remember, you can challenge yourself physically, take a social risk, learn a professional skill, or break a habit. Create an outline of how you might pursue these activities.

3. **Action:** Choose one of the activities you identified above and make it happen!

three

Who's That in the Mirror?

It's funny to think about the old me running around in this sheep's costume. It's actually more distressing than funny. And it's distressing because not only was I wearing a costume, I was also convinced that I actually was a sheep, not a wolf.

Obviously, I'm neither a sheep nor a wolf, but this is the metaphor I use when I try to explain the old me. When talking to groups about talents, strengths, values, and the benefits of embracing our unique qualities, I feel compelled to admit how difficult it was for me to see myself as I really was.

Just as I have encouraged you to take the Clifton StrengthsFinder® assessment (at the outset of this book and again in Chapter 2), I also encourage the individuals and employees whom I coach to do the same. I feel comfortable encouraging everyone and anyone to take this assessment, because learning my results had a profound impact on me.

The feedback I received was both shocking and completely accurate. Although my results surprised me immensely, I found that once I was able to digest the information and objectively consider how the findings could be used to my benefit, I was both heartened and relieved.

I could take the sheep's costume off and just be me.

The results came as a big shock because I thought I had nothing left to learn about myself. I'm someone who leans toward introspection and, what's more, as an organizational development professional, I'd taken more than my fair share of assessments over the years. But my Clifton StrengthsFinder® results were different from these other assessments whose findings seemed to be generic personality-related platitudes. In sharp contrast to what I had experienced in the past, the Clifton StrengthsFinder® "Top 5 Strengths" hit the nail on the head.

My results indicated that I have the following Strengths in the following order:

1. Competition
2. Maximizer
3. Achiever
4. Activator
5. Significance

It was the first one, Competition, that threw me at first. Most likely it was due to my belief that competitive women were hated, friendless creatures who slithered around like snakes in the grass. After college and graduate school, I quickly surmised that exposing my competitive nature would ostracize me from the world. In an academic setting, I felt comfortable going out strong for the win, but in the business world I completely lost my footing.

No woman needs to read Sheryl Sandberg's *Lean In* to recognize that highly competitive business women are commonly assumed to be narcissistic backstabbers. I certainly did not want to be associated with that image. I wanted to be thought of as a compassionate person who built up others. Given my strong belief about how competition worked against women in the workplace, it is understandable that I felt the need to metaphorically zip myself into the sheep's costume every day.

On a personal level, I also had negative associations with competitive women. My sister had a frenemy (friend + enemy = frenemy) I'll call Carol. Carol was constantly trying to one-up my sister on every possible level: how much money she made, how happy her kids were, how many miles she ran that morning. The list went on indefinitely.

I loved hearing the Competitive Carol stories because her need for affirmation and one-upping defied belief. We openly referred to her as Competitive Carol in every conversation, and thus the mean-spirited nickname became a running joke at Carol's unknowing expense.

The Competitive Carol stories only solidified how awful being a competitive woman was – not only was she clawing her way to the top at work, she was squashing others down with her competitiveness during her non-work hours. In my mind, the term competition, when used to portray a woman, meant someone who was desperate on many levels – for success, for attention, for affirmation.

I was sure that this horrific descriptor, Competitition, that sat at the very top of my StrengthsFinder® assessment MUST be a mistake. The nail in the coffin was my professional occupation. As a human resources consultant I wanted to be seen as a relationship builder and confidant. How could I ever be a professional or personal success if these competitive wolf-like tendencies were key parts of me being me?

Only after I learned the true Clifton StrengthsFinder® definition of Competition was I able to slowly accept that this descriptor accurately captured and explained a driving force inside me. The need for feedback and the desire to measure my progress are examples of what it REALLY means to be highly competitive. I had to disassociate the idea that being competitive meant that life was a zero-sum game and that high-Competition people all strive to win the game of life at the expense of others. I didn't want others to lose — as a Maximizer I want everyone to grow and get better.

On the flip side, when I honestly reflected on a few of my proudest moments and greatest personal triumphs, they were win-lose achievements. I guiltily realized that I was deserving of the label "competitive" as I assessed myself with a more open-minded understanding of what the term meant.

I quickly recognized that during periods of my life when clear achievements and success were lacking, I was miserable. Possibly my greatest struggle as a new mom and a novice business owner was the lack of feedback I had available to me to judge my progress. I missed having a report card or at least an annual review. The silence was deafening. I knew that my children's pediatrician wasn't going to tell me "These are the healthiest kids I've ever seen! My God, you're amazing!" since we were in the office for ear infections and stomach bugs as much as everyone else. And my clients paid me and thanked me, but their payment and comments seemed obligatory. I knew something was missing but I had no idea what I truly needed or how to get it.

Getting in the Arena

At the same time I craved positive feedback, I intensely feared criticism. And it was the fear of criticism that kept me from reaching for more – at home and at work. I refused to listen to my husband's encouragements and take his advice to get in the arena.

David's "getting in the arena" references were his shorthand way to summarize Theodore Roosevelt's famous quote delivered at the Sorbonne in 1910 about who and what really counts. Is it the critic or those who dare greatly?

It is not the critic who counts; not the man who points out how the strong man stumbles, or where the doer of deeds could have done them better. The credit belongs to the man who is actually in the arena, whose face is marred by dust and sweat and blood; who strives valiantly; who errs, who comes short again and again, because there is no effort without error and shortcoming; but who does actually strive to do the deeds; who knows great enthusiasms, the great devotions; who spends himself in a worthy cause; who at the best knows in the end the triumph of high achievement, and who at the worst, if he fails, at least fails while daring greatly, so that his place shall never be with those cold and timid souls who neither know victory nor defeat.

David wanted to inspire me and convey that the critics I so feared were of much less importance than anyone they might ridicule.

And it was David who threw me into the arena on one hot and humid day in August, 2008. The preceding summer, while touring the culinary arts building of the Indiana State Fair, David made a threat he'd made many times before. He claimed he would enter my banana bread in Indiana State Fair competition. "Ha, ha, you are SO funny!" I had ironically responded. But that year, after perusing the quilts and other handmade garments on the floor above, David wandered down to the basement and actually found the state fair employee who ran the entire culinary arts department. He proceeded to pick her brain. "How do you enter? Do the same people win every year? Did you know my wife makes great banana bread?"

Embarrassed, I shook-off the short Q & A and refused to believe that he might make good on his promise to sign me up the following year. I knew my banana bread was edible – and possibly even better than average – but it wasn't amazingly different, delicious, or unique. I recognized that my husband's love for my banana bread had more to do with his love for me than anything else. He was lovingly deluded into thinking that I could get in the arena with Indiana State Fair banana bread competitors and emerge a winner. I knew better.

The day David announced that he had actually entered my name in the banana bread competition at the Indiana State Fair, I almost became physically ill. Anticipating the plummet in store for me was brutal. As it stood, I had a recipe that wasn't special but was a family favorite. Given David's eagerness to test my culinary skills on a larger field, I would now be forced to expose myself to a larger, less loving, and thoroughly unbiased audience.

After a few weeks of hand wringing, I got to work perfecting the bread. Timing is everything with bread and I had to sharpen my baking time so that my processes were more scientific and less gut decision.

Dropping off my banana bread at the culinary arts building that momentous day in August was thoroughly anticlimactic. The State Fair employees who were checking-in all the baked goods (and looked to be seasoned culinary arts veterans) offered no words of praise or hints of reassurance. I was encouraged to return in 14 days to learn the fate of my bread. A Competitors' Reception was planned for the brave Indiana cooks who had entered into the cook-offs, and their proud family members.

Those 14 days passed slowly – like molasses slow – and I half wished my husband would forget the Competitors' Reception. No such luck. By 9 a.m. David was rallying the kids for our BIG day. "We get to see if mom won a blue ribbon tonight," he told them. I wanted to kick him in the shins. "Don't create false expectations!" I hissed.

Later that day I twisted my ankle, no doubt trying to fulfill my half-conscious desire to forgo our evening plans. Maybe I was in too much pain to go to the reception? No, I couldn't even convince myself that it was more than a minor sprain. I couldn't get off the hook that easily.

When the time came, I hobbled into the Indiana State Fair culinary arts building to look for my banana bread. The packed glass cases housed a bounty of home-cooked items: jams, pies, cakes, cookies, hard candies, yeast breads, sweet breads and so much more. Among the hundreds of items on display, it was not easy to find my bread that the judges had recently sliced and plated.

It was actually David who spied the bread before I did. Upon identifying it as my bread, he immediately hoisted his fists in the air – making the universal sign of victory. A blue ribbon lay next to my once lowly, now victorious, banana bread.

It's hard to explain just how good that victory felt. It was completely unexpected but remarkably validating. I could only guess what the cooking resumes of other competitors looked like, but I was proud to have beaten them fair and square.

Accepting my competitiveness has allowed me to push myself to new limits. For example, in the past I might have shied away from win-lose situations because "I didn't really care." Of course, in reality I cared so much that the pain of losing seemed like too much of a risk. **What I've realized is that the pain of NOT taking a leap and risking a loss is actually worse than losing.** I have started to own the fact that I want to win, even if I know that realistically I can't win all the time and in every situation.

What's Your Story?

The value of the blue ribbon cannot be monetized, because it is priceless to me. However, it may surprise you to learn that the much-cherished blue ribbon is not displayed in my home or office. It is happily tucked away in a folder in the depths of my poorly organized filing cabinet. I have no need to frame it, nor do I want to cast my eyes upon it but once every few years. And that is because the story is much more important than the ribbon.

The banana bread story gives me insight into myself and allows others to peek inside my internal highs and lows – my truest desires and greatest fears. I have used it in icebreakers, such as "Tell us a fun fact about yourself that no one knows"-type situations and frequently use it in presentations when illustrating how understanding and even accepting our strengths can take more introspection and honesty than one might initially think.

But the most valuable take-away that I have garnered from obtaining a blue ribbon and subsequently constructing a story around the sequence of events is that I have a go-to story about myself that is for myself. It is a story of risk and fear and ultimate success. It is a story that I can replay in my head when I am insecure or, alternatively, when I am on top of the world.

Psychologists have long known that the running commentaries — the stories — we tell ourselves are fully linked to our current confidence and future performance. If my silent self-talk says, "Sarah, you are a horrible disaster and a sad excuse for a baker," I will most likely feel terrible about myself and produce a baked product that is commensurate with my negative feelings. Given this understanding of the negative impact our pessimistic running commentaries and dour self-talk can have on us, it seems obvious that we should strive to eliminate the negative stories we tell ourselves about ourselves and install positive stories.

Unfortunately, patterns of thought are very hard to change. If we have been raised in an environment that feeds us these negative stories, it can be a huge struggle. However, it is a struggle that must be confronted and overcome. Why? Because the stakes just got higher. Research also tells us that it takes three positive comments to balance out the impact of one negative comment. Scientists who study this phenomenon call it the *Positivity*® *ratio*.

In his book *Before Happiness*, Shawn Achor[6] presents this research conducted by Marcial Losada and Barbara Fredrickson. Furthermore, studies have found that the highest performing work teams were found to have a 6:1 ratio, meaning that the best teams received six positive comments to every one negative comment. It seems reasonable to conclude that our internal dialogue should strive for a similar ratio.

If you cannot eliminate a negative story from your internal self-talk playlist, at least now you know that you need three positive stories waiting on the sidelines of your mind to counterbalance the effects of each negative one.

Luckily, your "Top 5 Strengths" can serve as guideposts for where to look for your stories. In my case, the banana bread story helps me remember that winning is important to me and that even when I think the odds are firmly stacked against me, I need to get in the arena.

What does your internal playlist look like? Do you have many reels going at once or one constant theme? Given this new understanding of self-talk and the Positivity® ratio, is it plausible that the stories you have told yourself in the past have been directly impacting your success or lack thereof?

Exercise: Create a Positive Story Playlist

1. What negative story or stories do you replay?

2. How can you eliminate or at least reduce the negative replays? Admitting to yourself that these stories exist and need to be diminished is a great first step.

   Second steps include trying to re-frame the negative situation into one that is more positive. If you say to yourself, "I'll never get this done, I'm not organized enough!" consider a less harsh perspective like, "This is a big project. It's going to take a lot of organization and I may need some advice."

3. Construct as many positive stories about yourself as you can muster in one sitting. List your "Top 5 Strengths" from your Clifton StrengthsFinder® assessment results and your top two values and start brainstorming. Any positive and authentic story about yourself is fair game. For example, if you have Woo in your Top 5 chances are that you are constantly winning people over (Woo stands for Win Over Others). When was the last time you made the server at a restaurant or checkout attendant at your grocery store smile?

The positive stories you have at your disposal may be things you consider "no big deal" since it's natural and easy for you to behave in that manner. You love to win over others (Woo), or figure out the best way to get things done (Strategic), or help others consider the historical perspective on a situation (Context). These are all examples of Strengths in action.

It is easy for you to use your Strengths, and that is exactly the point. The things you are best at – the positive traits you have and use every day – may be going unnoticed and underappreciated by you.

However, now that you know that you need at least three and as many as six positive stories to replay in your mind to outshine the one negative story, you may value yourself and your abilities more highly. I hope so.

Whenever I get feedback from workshop participants or students at the end of a semester, I eagerly look at my rating and the comments that go along with my scores. When I first started teaching, I always focused my attention on the lowest ratings, with the false notion that if I paid close attention to the negative comments, I would grow from the experience and improve my skills as an instructor. Honestly, it just upset me. My scores have improved over the years, but it has come from being more "me" and less worried about the critics.

I have come to realize that there will always be a workshop attendee or a student who gives me a score that is below the consensus of the group. It is unrealistic to assume that I can please everyone. Understanding the positivity ratio has played a critical role in my shift from focusing on the critics (whose scores and comments are very different from the majority) to objectively weighing the feedback of the entire group.

four

Change Ahead

Understanding one's Strengths, values, motivators, and vision are fundamental keys that open the door to becoming unstuck and feeling more complete. Your Strengths, values, and motivators have been there all along, but you have been unaware of their importance. Your vision for the future was clouded and blurry because you lacked internal clarity.

You may have shunned, downplayed, or devalued your Strengths and values because it was more important for you to get along with others or quickly get something accomplished than it was to make sure your voice was heard. However, without truly owning your uniqueness and the things that make you you – you end up living a lie. No one wants to live a lie.

Moving from a life that is filled with teeny tiny white lies, to a life where you stick up for your uniqueness is not easy. Trust me. Why is it is so hard? It's hard because change is disruptive and can be terribly difficult.

There are many reasons for resisting change. Below are three issues that are commonly discussed in organizational behavior literature.

1. We have other things to do. Completing commitments and demands that are immediately in front of us cause us to push the "change" items to the bottom of the list, day after day after day.

2. We fear the unknown. While a small segment of the population loves to dive into learning about the ramifications of the change, most of us feel a sense of comfort doing the same thing and behaving in predictable ways.

3. It may negatively impact how we fit into our current roles. In the world of organizational behavior we call this the person-organization fit. But the same concept applies to individuals who have non-organizational roles – like being a parent, volunteer, or spouse. Your fit is important to you, whether you are within an organization, a family, or a community.

The research is clear when it comes to who copes best with change: those who can tolerate a lack of clarity and structure, and who are optimistic, cope best.

Learning to accept change as an inevitable part of life may allow you to embrace the changes that exist in today's world. More importantly, learning how to best integrate your Strengths and values into your daily life and shift away from accommodating the needs of others should help you to feel more complete and unstuck.

I like to consider myself to be someone who is open to change. But every once in a while I'm hit head-on with evidence to the contrary. In fact, every time I update my phone with Apple's newest software I am left feeling like a hypocritical jerk.

My initial reaction to a recent iOS update was hatred. I missed the 'old' iOS. I was mad at myself for being so weak and dependent on the comforts of familiarity, but the reality was that I was not happy about the changes. How could it be that my head says "change and progress are good" but my heart says "this is uncomfortable, confusing, and bad"?

I feel sure that my encouraging you to embrace change is not the first time that you've received this advice. Change allows us to grow and develop. It expands our brains. It allows us to stay one step ahead of our competition or – at minimum – keeps us from being left in the dust. Still, we resist it.

My personal gripe with change is most consistent with the second reason listed – fearing the unknown. To more fully personalize this reason for hating change I would need to add, "I hate feeling idiotic and needing to ask others for help." I am not sure why asking for help is troubling for me. Possibly it is because needing help feels dependent and needy. I want to be independent and all-knowing, yet I know this is an impossibility.

I am impressed with Apple's ability to pull me and many others into the future. Because my number one strength is Competition, my fear of 'losing out' motivates me to install the latest software update. My Achiever then kicks in and ensures that I quickly learn what is needed. Relying on your Strengths to help you through change is a coaching tool I frequently use as a Gallup Certified Strengths Coach.

Using Your Strengths to Accept Change

Below is a list of the 10 most frequently occurring strengths (based on 8,689,762 respondents) and suggestions for how you can harness these strengths when dealing with change.

1. **Achiever** – Achievers are hard workers. You need to visualize each change as a race that you want to complete. It is

an opportunity to show others your ability to check things off your to-do list. Your determination and hard work need to be funneled into change-related goals.

2. **Responsibility** – Individuals with high Responsibility follow through on the things they say they will do. When change is inevitable, tell a trusted colleague, friend, or superior that you intend to be a leader in embracing this change. Visualize how you will own an upcoming change and become the "go-to" person for others who also want to embrace change.

3. **Learner** – Learners love to be on the forefront of change. Reading about the ramifications of a particular change or interviewing others who know about it are great tools for you to use.

4. **Relator** – Relators enjoy close and genuine friendships. Relators should ask a close friend to walk step-by-step with them through the change process. Having a partner will make any change more bearable for you.

5. **Strategic** – Those with Strategic talents enjoy trying out new processes but may resist changes that have not been well researched. Getting in on the ground floor of change is critical for you. Use your Strategic strengths to make mid-course corrections.

6. **Input** – High Input folks have helpful resources that make changes more bearable. Using the information or tools at your disposal is a win-win for all. As someone with Input, you are gratified by first collecting the knowledge, then using it to help individuals or groups.

7. **Harmony** – Having Harmony as a Strength allows you to remain at peace in the middle of chaos. You look for common ground and appreciate people who, like you,

avoid conflict. Your ability to appease those who are upset by changes is a helpful team-strengthening skill in times of change.

8. **Empathy** – High Empathy individuals are able to understand how change impacts others. You are able to put words to the feelings that others experience. Use your emotional intelligence to think about the personal benefits that change can facilitate. You may need to use your Empathy talents to explain to others – who do not have your insight – why there is resistance to change.

9. **Adaptability** – Having high Adaptability means that you are open to changes and expect them around every corner. Your willingness to embrace change makes every day different and exciting. Help others without your talent to adapt and respond to the needs of the situation.

10. **Maximizer** – As a Maximizer, you enjoy taking something good and making it even better. You think of change as an opportunity for improvement and share with others your perspective on how an upcoming change could translate into individual or group benefits. Then, you track the progress that is made.

I had the opportunity to coach an administrative assistant, Dianna, who was overcome with anxiety about a change that was quickly approaching. Her second-born and last to leave the nest daughter had been accepted to a college that was halfway across the country. My client was quick to tell me how close she was to her daughter and how involved she was in her life, especially in recent months when her daughter's sports activities and senior-year celebrations consumed most of her and her husband's time and focus.

This loving mom's greatest fear was that her relationship with her daughter would change – for the worse – after she left for college. She was clearly proud of the relationship she had developed with her daughter, and the thought of losing something she so obviously prized shook her to the core. Dianna's strengths of Input, Harmony, Consistency, Individualization, and Achiever needed to be tapped if Dianna was to successfully launch her daughter as she started her college career.

I suggested that Dianna initially tackle the problem with what I called "her lead foot." Dianna and I had just spent an hour discussing her love for collecting information, reading about issues that fascinated her, and subsequently using this knowledge to create a well-organized and systematic environment at work. These natural tendencies showed me how Dianna's Input and Consistency, Strengths that ranked first and third within her Clifton StrengthsFinder® "Top 5 Strengths", strongly influenced her behaviors.

When I asked Dianna if she would consider doing some research about mother-daughter relationships, she eagerly agreed. My hope was that she would find some books that relieved her fears, inspired hope, and even outlined some key steps to maintaining and strengthening her mother-daughter relationship. Dianna loved the idea of better understanding the issue in front of her, and it had not occurred to her to investigate this issue as she would have tried to solve a work-related problem. Looking for key steps that helped other mothers and daughters in transition could serve as rules for Dianna and her daughter to live by. I recognized that Dianna would embrace the concept of *rules* because rules help establish predictability and individuals, like Dianna, who have Consistency crave predictability, fairness, and order.

Tapping into your unique Strengths allows you to authentically embrace change. Change will be necessary for you to feel complete. In future chapters, we will revisit how using your Strengths to achieve any goal or objective is the best route to success.

Exercise: Strength-Based Change

1. Which two Strengths (of the five presented in your Clifton StrengthsFinder® results) and one value (of the first five listed in your VIA Character Strengths results) are least integrated into your life today?

2. Why might that be the case?

3. How can you start using one of these under-utilized Strengths to reawaken your more authentic self? For example: if you are high Competition but have shied away from competitive situations of late, what might be a first-step to express your competitive nature?

five

20/20 Vision

My second-grade teacher, Mrs. Cameron, was wise, calm, serious, remarkably artistic, and strict. She had a good heart but she was no softy. We knew we couldn't get away with much in her classroom since she had seen it all. She'd raised her own kids and taught for years. Her resume would have fallen into the pile of seasoned vets if she had ever thought to leave the small Episcopal day school where she taught God-fearing and mostly well-behaved children to look for a higher paying job at the public schools around us. But she would never have betrayed us that way. We knew she loved us deeply, even if her tough exterior made her true feelings hard to decipher.

In the fall of my second-grade year, soon after school began, it became clear to Mrs. Cameron that I could not see the blackboard from my assigned seat. Of course, I thought I could see it just fine. I needed to squint my eyes a bit more than everyone else and sit in the front row (I had been moved to one of the desks that was closest to the blackboard), but I was sure that my vision was the same as my classmates'. Mrs.

Cameron knew better. She came to realize that I was getting many math problems wrong and not because the new math concepts were too challenging but because I had copied them down incorrectly from the blackboard.

At the Back to School night, Mrs. Cameron told my parents that I needed to have my vision checked. They chuckled knowingly. Why did they laugh? Because they had discussed upon marriage that the chances of any of their children having good vision were slim to none. Both of them had terrible eyesight. They even joked that they were blind as bats. My father wore thick glasses and my mother lived in her hard contact lenses even though they frequently made her eyes water profusely.

My two older sisters had already been fitted for glasses. In my parents' minds I was just joining the family's tradition of needing corrected vision. I, on the other hand, was shocked. I wholeheartedly believed that I could see perfectly well.

That misguided conviction changed once I got my glasses. I vividly remember coming home from the doctor's office with my new glasses and being dumbfounded by how crisp and clear the leaves on the trees outside my bedroom window had become. I felt as though I could reach out of the window and pluck each leaf off. No longer did the tops of the trees look like green balls of fur that covered brown tree trunks. I drew pictures like that in art class, but now I realized how inaccurate I had been. I took my new glasses on and off repeatedly to see the new and the old versions of world – back and forth I went. Getting eyeglasses was truly a life-changing experience. Mrs. Cameron was, of course, right again. And I had her to thank for changing my world from blurry and inaccurate to brilliant and credible.

There were things I hated about wearing glasses. I hated having them steam up when I got too hot playing at recess. It was annoying how they slid down my nose and I had to constantly push them back into place. Of course, I did not really like the way they made me look. I was not overly vain in second grade but I had some sense that I was not quite as cute with my glasses on as off. My parents confirmed this by saying they "could not see my face as well" with my glasses on and encouraged me to take them off for pictures. Despite these downsides, the glasses were a new part of me and I was glad I had them. I could see the world as it really was and that was a real pleasure.

Self-Discovery Brings Clarity to Your World

Being able to see yourself as you really are by using the exercises and tools within this book might feel like a completely new world. It could feel like going from being legally blind to having 20/20 vision. It is also possible that the impact on you is a more subtle development, akin to going in for a vision check-up and getting an updated prescription. Either way, regardless of whether the impact has been life-changing or only moderately life-enhancing, improving your understanding of self impacts how you see the world.

I regularly coach individuals who enter the coaching process with very modest expectations about gaining any new insights about themselves. They, like my second-grade self who believed she could see perfectly well, believe that they have a fantastic understanding of their strengths and motivations, their values and vision. In sum, they wholeheartedly believe they know themselves well. By the third coaching session, this misconceived theory is usually debunked.

One of my favorite examples of this occurred when I coached a business owner, James, who has Individualization® in his "Top 5 Strengths." In our first meeting, James reviewed his strengths with me and confessed that he did not see how Individualization was a central theme in his life. James had his own definition of what it meant to be individualistic, and for whatever reason, he did not believe he showed the traits that represented this word. For this reason, I always encourage my clients to read, or re-read, the short definitions of their "Top 5 Strengths" and highlight the phrases that resonate most with them. Although the 34 Strengths that make up the results of Clifton StrengthsFinder® assessment may seem commonplace, the individual definitions may give you an entirely new perspective on terms like Context, Activator, Significance, Self-Assurance, Restorative, Command, and Discipline.

When James reread the definition of Individualization as defined by Gallup, he started to accept that he might have some of the characteristics discussed in the description. For example, he recognized that although he might not remember the first and last name of every employee, he always remembered something special about him or her. He was always able to remember his or her unique story.

He left our first meeting unsure of how this trait impacted others or made him especially capable as a business owner but returned to our second coaching session convinced of the importance that Individualization played is his life – as a business owner, as a husband, and as a father.

James had asked one of his newer employees what he thought of the results he had received after taking the Clifton StrengthsFinder® assessment, and his employee remarked that he wasn't sure he completely understood each of his "Top 5 Strengths" fully. James chimed in by explaining his mixed feelings about having Individualization in his "Top 5 Strengths." The new employee remarked, "Oh, I really see that in you! You're always asking me particular questions about myself that shows you remember my interests and think of me as an individual and not just some employee." For James this was a watershed moment.

By the end of our third coaching session, we joked that James's Individualization was his most dominant Strength. He used it constantly at work and at home. He recognized how some parents treat their children interchangeably, and how shocking and upsetting this was to him. He was keenly aware of how different his children were from one another and from every other child he had ever known. He realized how his parenting style and his wife's parenting style were different — and how that made them a better team. His ability to focus on the differences of others was a central part of who James was all along . . . but he was able to recognize this only after seeing his Clifton StrengthsFinder® results, getting some coaching, and looking for validation in his daily thoughts and activities.

My favorite example of James flexing his Individualization came after a half-day training with all of his employees. Each employee had received a Certificate of Strength describing the unique talents that he or she demonstrated at work and at home. James encouraged everyone at the meeting to display these certificates proudly in their workspace. James underscored the importance of showing off each certificate by allotting each employee twenty dollars to purchase a frame of his or her choice for the letter-sized certificates. It had occurred to him to purchase enough frames for the entire group and to distribute them at the training session, but he wanted each employee to pick a frame that was personally appealing. This example struck me as a bulls-eye example of Individualization in action – by the man who had originally questioned this trait's relevance in his daily habit.

When Strengths are Underappreciated

On the flip side, I have coached individuals who clearly recognize how their "Top 5 Strengths" show up in their lives, but they do not view all of their traits as positive. These are some of the comments I have heard when coaching:

"Oh, so you mean there's something good that can come from having Responsibility?" This comment came from a manager who felt she had been dumped on again and again by higher-ups who took advantage of her dedication and willingness to see challenging projects through to completion.

"No one around here likes me, because I have Deliberative as a Strength. They think I cannot make a decision." This sentiment was expressed by an individual who had known since she was a child that she had trouble making decisions quickly. When I helped her reframe how the talents she used when she was being Deliberative helped her colleagues think through various possibilities and most likely protected the company from jumping into (Activator®) new endeavors too quickly, she started to view her Deliberative characteristics in a more positive light.

"I'll never succeed in the corporate business world, because I have too much Empathy." One of my most gratifying individual coaching opportunities was with Kim, the individual quoted above, who believed all of her strengths – and especially her Empathy – made her weak. She could not see how her insight into others' emotions could help her in business.

Kim had taken the StrengthFinder® assessment more than a year before she started working with me but it soon became clear to me that she did not fully understand her results. She was desperately searching for a new job after a succession of short-lived positions that only reinforced her idea that she had little to offer the kind of organization she aspired to join.

Kim was like a wilted flower. She was beautiful – inside and out – but she desperately lacked the confidence and pride in her natural talents that are fundamental to a successful job search. Discussing the practical ways that her strengths of Empathy, Harmony, Developer, Consistency, and Restorative could be used to sell herself in an interview was like putting a wilted hydrangea stem in a cool bucket of water. Kim blossomed immediately once we homed in on her love for organized workspaces, checklists, problem solving, and people. Armed with the new awareness that her "Top 5 Strengths" made her a strong candidate for the office manager position she fiercely wanted, Kim returned for a second interview.

Immediately after the interview, Kim gave me a full report of how things went. She was almost giddy. Kim knew the interview had gone well and said it was a sharp contrast from her first interview that had taken place prior to our coaching sessions when she was unsure of her strengths. Kim was hired immediately. The position paid $10,000 more per year than her last position, but infinitely more important than Kim's fantastic compensation package was the shift in Kim's understanding of herself and her talents.

In three one-hour coaching sessions, Kim discovered how to explain what she does best and how her skills could be put to good use. After less than eight months in her new position of office manager, Kim was promoted. Kim had been organized, timely, and easy-going in her past jobs. However, in the other positions she had not articulated to her employer how she could put her natural talents to use. Her greatest assets were going unused and underappreciated by Kim and by her employers. Once Kim gained confidence in herself and acknowledged her abilities, she found a position that was well-suited for her and an employer who valued her skills.

In the exercises at the end of this chapter, I will ask you to explore if you and the people who know you best (at work and at home) **fully exploit your strengths**. Exploit is a strong word, but why wouldn't you want to fully utilize your talents?

Downsides?

Are there any downsides to knowing your Strengths, akin to the downsides I experienced when I wore glasses in second grade? Once I started to fully acknowledge the role my Strengths played in my life, I found great freedom and power devoting my time and energies to the things I do best. But I continue to have a hard time admitting to myself that I lack certain skills.

I love jumping into new projects and, conversely, have a hard time doing the same routine over and over. I enjoy seeing everyone as an individual and therefore, have difficulty treating everyone the same way. I wish I were better at creating and sticking to routines. But understanding my Strengths – and deficiencies – has helped me appreciate other people's talents more fully. In Chapter 7 we will discuss how finding Strengths Champions, people who understand and deeply appreciate the Strengths you bring, will create an environment that encourages you to be the best you that you can possibly be every single day.

Learning about my Strengths has changed the way I see myself and the world around me, just as getting my first pair of glasses vastly improved my ability to see the leaves on the trees with distinctness and accuracy. Mrs. Cameron was a great teacher because she caught the subtle – and not so subtle – clues that exposed my vision deficiencies. You may have thought up until recently that you knew yourself fairly well. I wonder what you have learned about yourself thus far on our journey together.

Exercise: Assessing Your Progress

1. What Strengths do you flex daily? This week, take time to record when you catch yourself using your Strengths. Use your daily calendar to note your Strengths achievements.

   For example:

   Achiever – got my to-do list done!

   Maximizer – pushed my son, daughter, husband, or wife to make an improvement

   Empathy – took time to listen to a colleague

   Responsibility – made the deadline for a customer

   Relator – spent time with family members

   Recording how your Strengths naturally show up in your life will give you more incentive to return to the well. Strengths-based activities are rewarding and rejuvenating as opposed to weakness-based activities that tend to make you feel as though you are hitting your head against a wall. It feels good when you stop performing weakness-based activities because you are depleted and de-energized after performing tasks that are far outside of your Strengths zone.

2. What are the pros and cons of seeing yourself more clearly? I have tried to touch upon many of the benefits that you will reap from being exactly who you are. However, as we covered in Chapter 4, change is hard. Why might it be

easier to see yourself the way others see you or the way you have seen yourself in the past?

Create a PROS and CONS list that enumerates the real or imagined benefits and detriments of being more authentic.

3. We are at the halfway point of this book. What have you learned about yourself so far? It is important to record the one or two "ah-ha" moments you have had while reading, writing, and contemplating, because it can be difficult to remember what our old belief system was once we shift to a new belief system.

This is referred to as the curse of knowledge. In one of my favorite books, *Made to Stick*, the authors, Dan and Chip Heath[1], explain that once we know something in great depth, we have a difficult time explaining it to someone else in a simple way. And actually this can happen when trying to remember how we used to think about ourselves and the world as well.

Writing a few words that summarize how and why your self-understanding is shifting may be invaluable to you in a few months' time when you want to reflect on what this process of introspection and self-discovery has allowed you to see more clearly.

Six

Frenemies
and Champions

As previously discussed, I love teaching organizational behavior concepts to college students. There are a number of reasons why I love this job, but my enthusiasm for teaching stems primarily from my conviction that the topics we examine and discuss in class are fully relevant to future professionals, and a good understanding of them will help my students to succeed. Occasionally, these topics are relevant to both the personal success and the professional success of my students. One such topic is navigating the tricky waters of office politics.

Although some students are surprised that skillfully maneuvering political issues at work is both necessary and ethical, once we hammer out the differences between ethical and unethical political tactics, there is a more thorough recognition of why that is the case. Ethical political tactics include networking, managing your impression, keeping informed, being positive, obtaining positive recommendations, and using sincere flattery. Of course, in the scope of my college course we discuss how these tactics can and should be used at work. But each of these positive political tactics can also be used in your personal life to create a well-established social network.

Unethical political tactics are decidedly more fun to discuss because instructor and students alike have acute memories of being zapped by at least one of these zingers. Negative and unethical political tactics include backstabbing, creating turf wars, placing a weak manager under you to help secure your position, and stealing credit – the most despised and prevalent unethical tactic of all. It is easy and fun to dramatize a few examples of unethical political tactics just to make sure my students get the drift.

Backstabbing is my hands-down favorite tactic to mimic since it allows me to relive being in eighth grade in a cathartic, if somewhat unhealthy, way. I preface my theatrical display of backstabbing by telling the class that they all remember seeing backstabbing occur in middle school. Then, I pick a student who is normally talkative and confident to serve as my victim in a dramatization of backstabbing in action.

I'll say "Oh my GOSH! I LOVE your shoes. So, so cool. Where did you get them? Super sparkly and cute!!" Anyone with a rudimentary understanding of backstabbing knows what has to come next. I turn to another student and say in a audible whisper "Oh my GOSH! Did you see her shoes? Awful! I mean terrible! What is she thinking with the sparkles?" Backstabbing is an immensely tempting skill to master at the tender age of thirteen when social dominance is everything and ethical behavior seems irrelevant.

Although the example is a prime example of claws-out catty eighth-grade-girl behavior, the skit is not lost on the men in the room. When the boys were in eighth grade, they witnessed many girls behaving this way and they experienced a similar form of backstabbing from their male counterparts. Given the flash-back feelings that are being experienced in the classroom, there is usually lots of laughter emitted regardless of the gender of the student.

The preceding example is intended to be a gut-wrenching trip down memory lane and, hopefully, a comical diversion from our lecture, but how does it play out at work? I usually give the following example using another pair of students to flesh out how backstabbing occurs frequently during our workdays. I'll say to another unsuspecting and silent role-playing student, "Wow, great presentation. Sam, I really learned a lot. Let me know how I can achieve some of those action plans you discussed. Congrats!" But just as in the prior example, I'll turn to another student and belittle the "colleague" I was just congratulating, "Ok, honestly, what did you think of Sam's presentation? I was so confused! He has a lot of work to do to make his idea lift off in an organization like this. Don't you agree?"

The backstabber is similar to the critic, referred to in the quote by President Roosevelt in Chapter 3. Seen from this perspective, the backstabber is considerably less brave and more despicable than the critic who Roosevelt claims is so unworthy that he or she "does not count." Why? Because the critic has, despite his inability to do anything other than criticize the action of someone else, at least taken a stand and claimed disapproval. The backstabber's cowardice is so strong that it prevents an honest confrontation to ensue.

Backstabbers lack self-confidence and, therefore, try to tear down others as a way to elevate themselves. The German term *schadenfreude*, defined as "pleasure derived from the misfortunes of others," comes to mind when such misguided thinking is considered. The backstabber gains when someone else loses. Conversely, the achievements, positive recognition, and good fortune of others are viewed as an unfavorable occurrence for the backstabber.

It is dangerous to spend time with backstabbers, because they fundamentally do not wish you well, do not enjoy your success, and firmly, if unconsciously, believe that your triumphs negatively impact them. And who would want to spend time with a backstabber anyway? Unfortunately, many of us.

Frenemy Defined

Frenemies, particular types of backstabbers, know us so well that they can cunningly deceive us into believing that they are our friend while simultaneously preying on our weakest link. Remember Competitive Carole from Chapter 4? She wanted to one-up my sister whenever the opportunity was possible. Competitive Carole is a textbook example of a frenemy.

The male frenemy commonly uses macho benchmarks to prove his superiority. Trophy wife, mcmansion, new car, the latest and greatest sports paraphernalia, and electronic gadgets are paraded around in an attempt to elevate himself in the eyes of his so-called friends. Men who look to crush their buddies in "friendly" sports competitions have frenemy tendencies.

Frenemies take pains to convince us that they care about us but, unlike true friends, frenemies have one or more of the following habits:

- Their words or actions frequently make you feel sad, less confident, or insecure.

- They are unable to apologize for unkind words or actions if confronted.

- They accuse you of being too sensitive.

- They enjoy telling you about plans that exclude you.

- If asked to describe you, they would note your weaknesses.

In short, frenemies pretend to be true friends but only because this closer vantage point allows them greater access to the vulnerabilities of others. Once they determine the weaknesses of their victim, they will expose these deficiencies and feel elevated due to their victim's demeaned status.

Champion Defined

A champion is the opposite of a frenemy and better than a run-of-the-mill friend. A champion is the kind of friend who can be counted on to not only bolster you during difficult times, but see the positive in you when you cannot. The champion is the friend you need when you are feeling wobbly and withdrawn, sad and unsure. A champion has one or more of the following habits:

- Their words or actions buoy your spirits and immediately lift your mood.

- They are sympathetic to your insecurities and worries and minimize them with their positive perspective.

- They appreciate the many facets of your personality.

- They are never jealous of other friendships or plans made that do not include them, nor do they try to illicit jealously from you.

- If asked to describe you, they would embarrass you by using only adjectives such as BRILLIANT, AMAZING, FAITHFUL, TRUSTED, HILARIOUS.

Given the stark differences between frenemies and champions, it is apparent that frenemies have no place in your unstuck life. Frenemies do not want you and your Strengths to shine, because this will lessen their hold on you. Unfortunately, skilled frenemies may burden you with guilt when they notice that you want to live a life that is fulfilling and complete.

Breaking Free

Allison, a young woman whom I coached, shared with me a poignant example of how frenemies can be like lice or bed bugs — once they permeate your life, they are difficult to extinguish. When I initially meet with a new client, I frequently ask what her friends might say if I asked them to describe her. I followed this questioning with Allison but was disheartened by her response of "boring, healthy and negative" as the three adjectives she thought her "friends" would use to best describe her.

When I pressed back and asked Allison if her friends were showing the qualities of true friendship to her, she conceded that they were not. She recognized that if she had caring and meaningful friendships, her friends would value her positive attributes of being "healthy, honest, brave, and grateful." Granted, she had just told me that her friends would note her healthy lifestyle, but she did not think they valued or esteemed her for having this trait.

Allison had clearly outgrown these friends whom she had had since high school. She no longer wanted to go bar hopping every night but felt that she needed to oversee her friends' activities, lest they get themselves into trouble. Allison's friends relied on her to be their watchdog and sober driver, but labeled her as boring and negative, since she was the sensible voice of reason at the beginning of each night out and the only one of the group who questioned their antics at the end of the evening.

Logically, Allison knew that she needed a new group of friends, but emotionally she felt trapped in these old relationships and guilty for wanting to be free from them. They were like bad habits – hard to break.

As discussed in Chapter 4, change is difficult. Changing friends has all the normal change-related problems presented in Chapter 4. In addition, this type of change is laden with negative and guilt-inducing emotions. The guilty voice inside Allison's head asked her, "Do I think I am better than my old friends?" "Why couldn't I relax and have more fun?" And, "Who cares if my friends get a little bit wild at the bars?" It was the voice of her friends talking, not Allison.

After our third coaching session Allison reported that she was spending less and less time with her old friends and that her guilty feelings related to ending these negative relationships were subsiding. Allison was embracing her gifts and wanted to surround herself with friends who similarly appreciated her talents fully. I was greatly impressed by Allison's ability to address her frenemy relationships over the course of a month or two.

In the exercises at the end of this chapter you will be asked to consider the role you play in your frenemy relationship(s). This analysis is a great first step on the path to extracting yourself from the negative and limiting shadow your frenemies cast over your world.

As a child and as an adult, I chose frenemies who seemed powerful and all-knowing. Hiding my competitiveness was essential for me to survive in these relationships, because my frenemies were natural-born winners who did not want to share the limelight with me or anyone else. I was relegated to the role of cheerleader and adoring fan. Gaining a firm appreciation for my competitive spirit has helped me to step outside of the obscurity and darkness of my past frenemies' shadows.

Replacing the frenemies in your life with champions is not a short-term project. The first step in the process is self-recognition and appreciation of your unique self. Friends who cherish you for your authentic gifts remind you to nurture and grow these gifts. **It might take years to accumulate a band of champions** whom you can rely upon to help you weather the storms that roll through, and wholeheartedly celebrate the joyous events that dawn, **but it's worth the wait.**

Exercise: Discovering Champions

1. List the frenemies you have had throughout your life. What kept you or keeps you in frenemy relationships? What role do you play? (For example, I realized that I was playing the role of adoring fan in my frenemy relationships only after I more clearly understood how I was underusing my Competition).

2. Who are your champions? Again, start in grade school or earlier. List the teachers, friends, and acquaintances who have made you feel good about yourself.

   Are there particular moments with your champions – comments or written notes from them – that are seared in your memory as especially gratifying? Create a list that explains these occasions in detail.

3. How is your time currently allocated? Do you spend too much of your time with frenemies? Is it possible to reduce the amount of time you spend with people who do not

cherish you or the talents you bring? How would you make that happen?

seven

Lead by Recognizing the Strengths of Others

Recognizing the Strengths of others allows you to become a champion for the people in your life. As you become more and more sure about the unique talents you bring to the world, an uncanny phenomenon begins to occur related to how you see the people around you. Their talents and distinct abilities become more and more clear to you as well.

Exceptional leaders are able to detect the special gifts of others, because leaders are clear about what they, personally, have to offer. A leader in this sense does not necessarily mean a business owner, an executive, a person of political importance, or an individual who oversees the work of many people. It refers to someone who is influential. If leadership is understood in this way, we all have the opportunity to lead, because everyone has the opportunity to influence the people around them in a positive way.

You can and will become a Strengths-based leader if you work through the exercises in this book and fully accept your unique talents and gifts. Once you gain greater confidence about your assets, you naturally become less insecure about your deficiencies and therefore are more open to appreciating the talents of others with greater enthusiasm.

It is not necessary to have access to a person's "Top 5 Strengths" from the Clifton StrengthsFinder® assessment to become a Strengths-based leader. It wouldn't hurt, but it certainly isn't mandatory. Instead, start looking for signs of increased ability, engagement, and passion from the people you interact with on a daily basis. The positive traits of ability, engagement, and passion are clear signals that a person's talents are being utilized.

The most direct way to become a Strengths-based leader is to thank others for their commitment, effort, and hard work. Saying thanks to a friend, family member, colleague, or boss is a straightforward tactic and not overly demanding of your time and energy. Writing a thank-you note can take slightly more time and thought than extending thanks orally, but is not supremely taxing, right? Then what's holding you back?

Research indicates that only 10% of adults say thanks to a colleague every day, and just 7% express gratitude to a boss. Sue Shellenbarger reported these findings in her *Wall Street Journal* blog[1] and then went on to present the case for managers upping the praise quota in the workplace.

As we know from Chapter 5, the *positivity ratio* tells us that it takes three positive interactions to offset the impact of one negative interaction. For this reason alone, I agree with Shellenbarger's idea that giving thanks to others on a daily basis should be the norm and not the exception, but I question why the burden of praising others more frequently must be taken on solely by managers.

Regularly and sincerely showing appreciation for your colleagues, family members, and friends is an inexpensive and effective way to become a positive and influential person in someone's life. In short, it allows you to lead others as well as to become their champion.

Leading by focusing on what others do best is also a critical trait of a servant leader. The concept of serving others as a means to leadership has been discussed in religious teachings for centuries. However, it was Robert Greenleaf who coined the term *servant leadership* when he introduced the topic in his 1970 article "The Servant as Leader"[3] and applied this term to business leaders as well as social and religious leaders. Greenleaf's writings about the characteristics of a servant leader are consistent with what I have attempted to discuss here related to finding a champion for yourself and being a champion of others.

I am always energized when I have the opportunity to coach individuals with natural leadership abilities. As a Maximizer, I love taking clients from good to great and exposing how they can quickly gain speed by capitalizing on their Strengths. It doesn't matter what their "Top 5 Strengths" are. There isn't a magic combination of Strengths that invariably make fantastic leaders, but great leaders share excellent insight about self and others.

Kodee, a young manager with 16 direct reports, is a prime example of someone who is a successful manager because she understands and takes advantage of the best qualities in herself and her team members. Kodee has Maximizer, Relator, and Significance in her "Top 5 Strengths." She told me that she loved her job because she helped her staff be more than they could even imagine (Maximizer). She insisted on promoting authentic and meaningful relationships with this group (Relator), despite the obstacle of having more than half of her staff in remote locations. Finally, Kodee was candid with me and admitted that she enjoyed being a key person in the eyes of others. She wanted to be admired and simultaneously felt the keen need to pull others forward (Significance).

Kodee's self-reported leadership abilities matched the words that her teammates used to describe her – in some cases verbatim. After two coaching meetings with Kodee, I was asked to coach all 16 of Kodee's direct reports. Their glowing accounts of how Kodee "goes to bat for me," "expects the best from me and therefore, I give her the best," and "helps me surpass my dreams," validated my suspicion that Kodee was a champion and servant leader through and through.

Accept the "Daily Thanks" Challenge

I challenge you to give daily words or notes of thanks to the people you see regularly – from the grounds keeper at your office, to your spouse, to your best friend. At best, if you choose to accept this challenge, you could trigger a cultural shift and a positive ripple effect of gratitude and thanks that radiates out from you and into the various human networks to which you belong. If each of the people you thank decides to mimic your behavior, you could create a tipping point of gratitude in your organization, in your family, or in your group of friends.

At minimum, if your actions just make a few people smile, you will have improved the mood of someone for hours after your kind words have been given.

Ideally, those of you who accept the "Daily Thanks" challenge will become preoccupied with looking for the good in others and the world around you. Positive psychologists call this the *positive tetris effect*. Shawn Achor, in his book *The Happiness Advantage,*[6] encourages individuals to positively train their brain to look for the positive, because this focus will allow them to see more positive things and ultimately improve their mood.

This does NOT mean becoming oblivious to the negative, sad, or troubling issues that rub up against us daily. It means learning to take the time needed to shift your focus and perspective in order to fully appreciate the good in your life. This positive shift can increase your creativity, lower your stress, and even help you to complete your goals.

Of course, the opposite of the positive tetris effect is the negative tetris effect – the phenomenon of only looking for negative and gloomy things to focus your attention upon. The negative tetris effect has the opposite impact on your life. As illogical and sad as it might seem, many individuals are prone to this type of thinking. They have trained themselves to look for the negative and their pessimism has an adverse impact on their happiness and abilities. Research has found that those individuals with a negative mindset have greater chances for depression, stress, and even substance abuse.

The rationale for taking the "Daily Thanks" challenge is simple: why not? The potential benefits to you and others are far-reaching. Below are some do's and don'ts for looking for the positive and giving thanks to those whom you appreciate:

Do's

1. Make it a habit. Commit to saying thanks or writing a quick note to someone – anyone – every single day. Habits are hard to form but, once formed, can have an enormous impact on personal performance. To form a strong habit you need a cue to help trigger your behavior and a reward to condition yourself to enjoy the new habit. For example, a cue could include your morning coffee, a mid-day e-mail check, or an end-of-day organization of your desk. Rewards that fit nicely with these examples include enjoying your morning coffee, partaking in a quick call to a loved one, or appreciating your orderly work station. Once you

make a new routine, you will anticipate the good feelings of your reward, and it will become automatic for you to thank someone every day.

2. Use various forms of communication – spoken, hand-written, text, e-mail. Mix it up, and eventually you will find a preferred thanking style. I gravitate toward the hand-written note and keep a stash of inexpensive cards in my glove compartment and desk drawer for exactly this purpose.

3. Tell someone about your "Daily Thanks" challenge. This may seem a bit do-goody and show-offish for some. Choose the person you plan to tell with care – someone who won't be threatened but might be inspired. You want to be held accountable, and even if the person who knows about your plans to thank others daily does not follow-up about this new habit, you will feel more committed by verbalizing your commitment and intentions.

Don'ts

1. **Be insincere.** Insincere thanks can be sniffed out a mile away. Focus your attention on the acts of helpfulness, kindness, hard work, commitment, or humor that genuinely impress you.

2. **Be backhanded.** Don't give thanks to someone while also including a jab. "Despite your flubbing up Harrison's first name, you pulled off a great presentation" is a back-handed compliment. It takes some humility to thank someone sincerely. If backhanded compliments are a habit of yours, consider what motivates your phrasing. Nerv-ousness or fear of looking emasculated and overly tender-hearted can prompt poor thanking skills. Be aware of your tendencies and try to improve your skills by modeling

those who have a knack for simple and to-the-point compliments.

3. **Forget the obvious.** Complimenting people on their glaringly obvious gifts is encouraged. It might seem silly and self-evident to point out how detail-oriented and dedicated your accountant is or how easy to talk to and warmhearted your priest seems with everyone he encounters. It's not. Although someone's gifts might be clear to you, it's not silly to continually compliment people about their unique skills. In fact, all of us love to receive compliments of the same kind over time because it reinforces our natural desire to use our talents.

I was coaching a group of college admissions personnel who worked for a Catholic university. Father Joe, a Catholic priest and member of this team, had talents that were consistent with someone who cared deeply for people. When I asked Father Joe if he ever got tired of getting compliments about how kind and helpful he was to students, colleagues, and friends, he said "NEVER!" I wanted to see if at some point the compliments might get overwhelming. "But Father, would 50 compliments a day be too many?" He replied, "NO!"

Even priests enjoy being complimented for the work that they do well. It is not an indicator of weakness or vanity. Don't forget to reinforce the obvious talents of others because frequently it is those compliments that resonate most with the recipient.

Exercise: Becoming a Strengths Leader and Champion

1. Partaking in a mental review of the compliments you have received in the past may give you insight into what types of praise carry the biggest punch for you. After some solo brainstorming, create a list of the best compliments you have ever received.

2. Rate your ability to give praise. Is it easy for you or challenging? Why might that be the case? Some individuals believe that praise should be doled out sparingly to make it more impactful. How would you rate yourself on a scale from 1 to 10, if a 1 was "Rarely Praise Others" and a 10 was "Constantly Praise Others"? Who or what incidents might have shaped your outlook on praise?

3. Praising the process, not the outcome, is very important and can require a shift in attention. If you decide to take the "Daily Thanks" Challenge, make an effort to compliment the effort and commitment of others, not just the end result.

   For example, if your child studies diligently and gets an "A" on a math test, you should praise the hard work that went into studying for the test, not just the result. If the child, spouse, or employee is taught that only the end result matters (for example, getting an "A", winning the game, selling the contract) they will be more likely to play it safe in the future.

   When the outcome, not the productive process, is the only measure of success and the focal point of praise, the full potential of the individual can be limited. Highlight the process it took to get the "A", win the game, and sell the contract to encourage growth and development in those around you.

eight

Perspective Is Everything

Perspective is important in life and in art. It took more than a few thousand years of civilized living and drawing until the concept of perspective made its way into artistic drawings around the year 1400. This was about the same time that cartographers were making maps of the entire world with more detail and accuracy.

It is possible that the issue of perspective is of greater importance to you today than it was when you first picked up this book. If that's the case, the reason for this is because you have a greater understanding of your personal perspective on the world, a bit like the mapmakers came to have in the 15th century. An improved understanding of your unique perspective- – a compilation of your Strengths, motivators, values, and vision – is fundamental to becoming unstuck.

We become stuck when we lose sight of our unique and completely personal perspective. We may pretend to enjoy doing things that do not fully interest or excite us. We may pretend to care about things that do not stir us deeply. We may pretend to have the same vision of the future as our loved ones, colleagues, or boss. We hide our true perspective because we believe it is easier. We don't want to ruffle feathers, cause a fuss, or insist on being different.

In the short term, the habit of pretending to be more like those around us may reduce conflict with others. However, being inauthentic by ignoring our uniqueness creates internal conflict. Whether the pages in this book have allowed you to recognize your unique perspective for the first time or merely refocus your energies on the things that matter most to you, the goal thus far had been to reacquaint yourself with the authentic you that has been there all along.

Blind Spot

When decisions need to be made or projects need to be accomplished, it can be immensely helpful to seek the perspective of someone else. In fact, accepting your unique perspective should spark an awareness that obtaining one or more perspectives different from your own can help you avoid being blindsided.

All of us have blind spots that prevent us from seeing things from a particular vantage point. Physically, it is easy to understand that you cannot see, without the use of mirrors, the middle of your back. Even those of us who are mothers do not literally have eyes in the back of our heads.

Accepting that you cannot see some things easily – or in other words, admitting that you have a blind spot – is helpful to the un-sticking process. The bad and good result of this admission is that you must rely on others. Once I was able to step away from the false notion that I could or should be all-knowing, I was able to ask for help from others and appreciate their perspectives.

Productive Partnerships

The most productive partnerships arise when individuals find the yin to their yang – a person who can see what the other cannot. And the term "find" is intentionally used instead of "look for" or "search for," because productive partnerships are uncovered much like an archeologist unearths a wonderful artifact. It is a discovery process. When we discover people who seem to "fit" with us perfectly, we are amazed that they have different insights from us, yet make so much sense.

In most cases, we don't know exactly what we are looking for in an insightful partner. We cannot articulate how someone might be able to help us with our blind spot, or even the broad qualities that they might need, but when we find that person, we latch onto him.

This may be the case of how you found your spouse or best friend. For example, I coached a wonderfully dynamic couple, two business owners who are remarkably compatible, yet have very different strengths. Martin is a strategy guru – someone who sees a clear vision for the future (Futuristic) and enjoys contemplating the well-researched alternatives to get to that future (Ideation and Input). Martin's strengths are the yin to his wife's yang.

Anne-Marie, Martin's wife, is a Southern charmer who can win over young and old, rich and poor alike. It's a sight to behold. Her Woo (win over others) is like a pistol in her side holster, ready to be pulled at a moment's notice. She combines her Woo with her remarkable abilities of being able to talk her way out of a corner (Communication) and jump into new ventures quicker than you can say, "Let's do it" (Activator).

These two people have very different strengths, yet they are immensely compatible. When they met in their twenties, they did not consciously know what they needed in a life mate. But very soon after they started dating, they realized that they were meant to be together forever. Martin sees the plan that is invisible to Anne-Marie. Anne-Marie persuasively suggests new activities to Martin that might never have occurred to him if it were not for his wife's positive spirit (Positivity) and impatience to get going (Activator). **Each compensates for the other's blind spot.**

Learning to value the perspective of our work colleagues can occur in much the same way. Initially, we may not know that our perspective is unique or, more importantly, facing directly at the blind spot of one of our work pals. But it is these insights that ultimately create the most productive partnerships.

Below are a number of possible partnerships that create mutually insightful relationships.

Activator who says, "Let's go!" VERSUS **Intellection who says, "Let's think!"**

Adaptability who says, "I love change!" VERSUS **Discipline who says, "I love Consistency!"**

Connectedness who says, "I love the mystery in the world!" VERSUS **Analytical who says, "I love understanding the proven truths of the world."**

Context who says, "I love the historical perspective!" VERSUS **Futuristic who says, "I love imagining what could be!"**

The possible options are numerous, but the point is that we each have a yin to someone else's yang. Accepting an alternative perspective, one that is diametrically opposed to our unique and personal perspective, is critical for our ultimate success and ability to become unstuck.

In the Wrong Place

Have you ever felt as though your perspective was not embraced by those around you? What if: (1) you see the world very clearly from your perspective; (2) your perspective sheds light and insight on the issues that seem to be the blind spots of those around you; but (3) the feedback you receive from others is, "Sorry, I don't understand/value/want your viewpoint."

Sadly, you may be in the wrong place at the wrong time. It can be maddening and frustrating to feel you have a perspective that is desperately needed, only to realize that it is a perspective that is not embraced. Instead of becoming unhinged by the craziness of the situation, liberate yourself — flee as fast as you can. There is a freedom that comes from realizing that you are in the wrong place at the wrong time, because you no longer need to try to explain your insights to an unappreciative audience or blame yourself for not being clear enough. **You can walk away.**

Jim, a smart and energetic individual, hired me while he was working full-time for a successful law firm as an office manager and pursing his MBA. At work, Jim wore multiple hats: recruiter, financial advisor, and go-to person for the large and small needs of multiple attorneys.

As an Arranger, Jim enjoyed being pulled in many directions at once. He used his Woo and Achiever to keep connected to his colleagues and impress them with his work ethic. Although three of Jim's Strengths were being tapped into daily, his top two Strengths of Strategic and Maximizer were languishing. After successfully reorganizing the law firm's non-attorney personnel, Jim longed to use his marketing abilities to take the small and successful law firm to the next level.

After a number of conversations with the firm's managing attorneys about gradually shifting his responsibilities toward marketing, it became clear that his notions of promoting and marketing the firm's market niche were not welcomed by the firm's decision makers. Historically, the law firm had not engaged in marketing campaigns and it did not see the benefit of adopting a new approach.

As Jim and I worked together to more fully realize his unique gifts and he started to 'flex his strengths more intentionally, Jim came to see that he was soon going to outgrow his office manager position. Although the managing partners of the firm were extraordinarily complimentary of many of Jim's skills, their discouraging words regarding his strategic marketing ideas were the writing on the wall regarding Jim's long-range plan for his career with the firm.

Jim's superiors did not welcome his strategic vantage point. The managing partners wanted to "do things as they always had," which meant they would employ no marketing strategy whatsoever. They did not want to consider that this perspective might be in the middle of their blind spot.

After the initial disappointment wore off, Jim realized that it was better for his long-term professional health to leave the firm within the next eighteen months. He was not running for the door, but he refused to bang his head against the wall, hoping that his novel marketing ideas would be incorporated into the firm's time-tested strategy of having no strategy. Jim had come to realize that he wanted to work where he was appreciated for ALL his talents. After this realization, he was able to funnel all of his strategic energies into finding a position and an organization that could provide the best fit.

Perspective Abuse

Why is the character Michael Scott, from the television show *The Office*,[1] such an amusing characterization of the world's worst boss? Possibly, it is because he is completely oblivious to his weaknesses. His lack of perspective is shocking. His arrogance is absurd. He believes that he has the deep respect of those who work for him when, in fact, they jeer at his incompetence and grandiosity. A classic Michael Scott quote that sums up both his lack of perspective and inflated ego is, "Would I rather be feared or loved? Easy. Both."

Fictional television characters are allowed – and encouraged – to have enormous personality flaws. These flaws can make them funnier to watch, more annoying to other characters on the show, and certainly more memorable to the viewer. But what happens when life imitates art? Is it hilarious or just insufferable to have someone in your life who lacks perspective? Easy. Just insufferable.

When talking to groups about harnessing their Strengths, I frequently discuss the troubles that occur when talents are overused. We lose perspective when we overuse our talents, because we no longer value differing opinions. To make matters worse, we can become oppressive and judgmental when trying to persuade others to see our side.

Everyone should have a healthy fear of losing perspective. As we come to appreciate our personal and unique perspective, our respect for the perspective of others should grow, not shrink. If we find ourselves becoming defensive about our actions or positions, it could be a clue that our perspective is out of focus.

A colleague, Nate, shared a story with me that captured how one person's lack of perspective can disrupt a team or training event. Nate frequently gives half- and full-day seminars to groups of individuals who do not know one another prior to their training day. Nate recounted how at a recent training event one of his participants went into self-promotion mode. Upon entering the room he introduced himself to everyone, distributed his business cards to all in attendance, and placed his remaining business cards in the empty chairs. As you can imagine, these tactics were met coolly by the other attendees.

Certainly, at a marketing event or a meeting that is solely for card swapping, his actions were appropriate. However, this was not the case. His actions lacked an awareness of the needs or interests of the other parties. In the end, forcing his business cards on everyone in the room, without establishing some rapport with the other attendees, came off as self-serving, competitive (in the bad way), and egotistical.

When our perspective is out of focus, when we come on too strong, when we try too hard, and when we KNOW we are right, we lose. The self-promoter in this story is an excellent example of someone who failed to see the perspective of others and subsequently failed to obtain his goal. Although I don't know with certainty what happened to the business cards that were distributed, my guess is that they were quickly thrown away by the other attendees.

Consider what might have happened with a gentler approach that shows an awareness of the perspective of others. Had the self-promoter waited until the end of the seminar to exchange cards with the people he found engaging, instead of merely dispensing his cards without genuine interest in the other attendees or showing reciprocity by obtaining their cards, he might have made a few lasting connections.

Exercise: Yin and Yang Together at Last

1. Can you identify one or more of your blind spots? When have you been blindsided in the past? As discussed earlier in this chapter, your blind spot could be the opposite of one of your strengths. As an Activator, I love to jump into

new things, but I can be blindsided by unforeseen complications.

2. Can you create partnerships that compensate for some of your bind spots? You may already have informal partnerships of this nature in place. Consider how certain friends or loved ones support you in various ways. Sometimes the most difficult advice to consider is the most important advice to hear. Other times, there is great relief in knowing that our partner can serve us by being the eyes in the back of our head, removing our blind spot.

3. Are you appreciated at work and at home for your unique talents? How could you expand the use of your Strengths in every area of your life? Do you fear you are in the wrong place at the wrong time? What evidence supports this suspicion?

4. Does someone around you abuse his perspective? Do you ever lack perspective? When is the last time you became defensive? Who were you with and what topic sparked your defensiveness? How can you become more open to the perspective of others?

nine

Get Gritty

Paul Tough's book *How Children Succeed: Grit, Curiosity, and the Hidden Power of Character*[1] is not just a great read for those who are interested in finding answers to the educational questions that plague our country – it's fantastic reading for those who are curious about predicting the success of people of any age. Tough pools research from an array of discipline. He consulted with economists, neuroscientists, psychologists, medical doctors, and teachers across the country to unlock the complex issue of how such character traits as perseverance, curiosity, conscientiousness, optimism, and self-control impact a child's future. Most importantly, Tough explains how these traits can be nurtured in children to better prepare them for the future and make them successful adults.

But how are the predictors of success in children different from those of adults? Tough does not examine these gaps. However, I suspect that there are many more similarities than there are differences. I would also suggest that more than a normal dose of grit is needed to become unstuck.

How Gritty Are You?

As the title of the book indicates, the three issues that Tough dives deeply into are grit, curiosity, character. Grit, in particular, interests me. It is an enchanting concept because it has an intuitive appeal and is gaining a foothold in the academic world. When I think of the word grit, I think of someone who is tough and tenacious. In my mind, there is a bulldog-type quality to someone who has grit. But how do psychologists define grit? A.L. Duckworth and her colleagues at the University of Pennsylvania[2] use the following definition when pursuing their work on grit: a "self-discipline wedded to a dedicated pursuit of a goal."

Duckworth has created a 12-item grit assessment that anyone can take free of charge.

An example of one of the items is:

I finish whatever I begin.

o   Very much like me

o   Mostly like me

o   Somewhat like me

o   Not much like me

o   Not like me at all

Take the full assessment and get feedback about your grittiness at **www.unstuckatlast.com/resources**.

It will become immediately apparent to you, if you decide to read through the entire questionnaire, that your results are only as accurate as your ability to objectively and honestly answer the questions asked. The instructions indicate that there are "no wrong answers" but a savvy assessment taker can quickly deduce the "best" responses if her goal is to obtain a score that indicates she is "extremely gritty."

To personally deduce your grit, without the use of the questionnaire, you could reflect upon interview-like questions, such as, "Have you ever had a goal that took you years to complete? What kept you on track and committed to completing your goal?" or "How do you react to setbacks? Can you recollect a setback you have had in the last year? How did you respond to it?"

Grit and Goals

Grit is needed for any goal that is worthy of being accomplished. Can you keep your eye on your goal and bounce back up after you receive a blow to your ego or an unforeseen obstacle arises? Duckworth's research found that the amount of grit an eighth-grade student has is the best indicator of future grades. Grittiness (as measured by self-discipline scores) was a better predictor of that child's eighth-grade GPA than the child's IQ scores.

Below is a list of common adult-centered goals and the gritty attitude that can help to make that goal a reality.

Goal	Gritty Attitude
Lose weight	I will not obsess over a small lapse. If I flounder, I will discontinue poor eating habits and start fresh tomorrow.
Reduce stress	Stressful days cannot be avoided. I will make every effort to handle them better and learn from my prior mistakes.
Save money	To achieve my goal, I will handle unforeseen expenses as they arise and dedi-

	cate myself to saving as much money as possible. If there is a month when I do not meet my goal, I will redouble my efforts in following month.
Obtain a degree	I will work to stay focused on my studies. If a required class is not of great interest to me, I will view it as a necessary part of my greater goal.
Stay in touch	I will be an authentic and reliable friend, spouse, child, or parent to others. When my life gets busy, I will remember that connecting to the people I care about gives me more energy and a greater sense of purpose.

The gritty attitude examples above can be used as a mantra and should be repeated at will over the course of your quest to make your goal a reality.

Gritty Interviews

I highly recommend that interviews contain at least one question that allows the job seeker to prove his grit. Uncovering the grit of your candidate, may be more important than a tedious analysis of his professional and academic qualifications. And here is a recommendation to job seekers: come up with a gritty story that can be worked into your interview, even if a direct question about grit is not posed. Your gritty determination will allow you to shine.

An example from many years ago shows how grit can be incorporated into the interview process even when the interviewer is not specifically asking about it. The interviewer in this case was me and the gritty interviewee, Karen, was applying for a Training and Development Director position in the Human Resources department where I worked. Karen's resume was impressive, but she did not have great depth of experience in the training and development field. In fact, her greatest achievement – having a PhD in English – seemed completely unrelated to the field she wanted to pursue.

And this is where Karen separated herself from the other candidates. When asked about her PhD in English, Karen explained that, "it was a result of stubbornness, more than anything." She further explained that after setting out on a path to obtain a PhD, she was not going to give up. She credited her grit and determination as the element that allowed her to complete her thesis – a feat many fall short of achieving.

In many ways, having a PhD could have been considered a strike against her at an organization such as this that valued masculinity and calloused hands over college degrees and book smarts. Ironically, it was her remarkable intellect that allowed her to reframe her qualifications in terms of grit – and that reframing won her many admirers in the interview process, and the job she sought.

Gritty Movie Characters and Historical Figures

Hollywood producers know that the American people love a story depicting a little guy beating the odds. We enjoy seeing others achieve their dreams even when the odds seem insurmountable. These are stories of grit. *Rudy*[3], the 1993 movie of a young man whose great dream was to attend and play football for the University of Notre Dame, is an excellent example of glamorizing grit. Rudy was small in stature and lacking a strong academic record but overcame these challenges and proved the naysayers – including family members, neighbors, and teachers who questioned his determination - wrong. Although the odds were stacked against him, Rudy was able to accomplish his goal of dressing for a Notre Dame game his senior year.

We leave inspiring movies, like *Rudy*, feeling as though anything is possible. These movies help us to hang on to the belief that the American Dream is not just a dream. Americans want to believe that anything is possible with hard work and determination.

I am a huge Abraham Lincoln fan due in large part to his remarkable success in the face of enormous adversity. Prior to becoming President of the United States he had lost eight elections and failed twice in business. His tenacity, his grit, is what inspires me to learn more about this remarkable man who overcame poverty, lack of formal education, heartbreak, the death of two sons, and a staggering debt to become the most written about figure in American history.

Getting Gritty with Your Strengths

The beauty of combining a gritty attitude with your unique Strengths is that an activity that once seemed painfully unsuited to your abilities can be transformed into an endeavor that is delightfully rewarding. It sounds a bit far-fetched, but the following example shows how one of my coaching clients turned mundane chores into rewarding accomplishments.

When I first met Jared, he was phasing out of his IT position with his long-time employer while funneling most of his energies into his new business. As can be imagined, Jared had many irons in the fire and very little free time. He resented using his down-time on weekends to do mundane tasks around the house when he wanted to spend this time doing things he loved to do, such as going on long bike rides with his wife.

Jared needed to use all of his Strengths to put a plan together for his home life, much like he had used these talents to mastermind his new business. Once we talked through the process and it dawned on Jared that his Strategic and Achiever Strengths could be put to good use in this way, he was off and running.

First, Jared needed to strategically consider his goals for the week. Then, he needed to make a weekly plan that included a checklist of items to get done daily. This checklist would ensure that Jared was moving key projects forward at work, exercising, completing household chores, and enjoying some recreational time with his wife every week. Given Jared's Ideation, he also needed to set aside time to think and contemplate. We recognized that this thinking time was critical for Jared to feel balanced and productive. As funny as it sounds, Jared needed to use his Strategic to make time for his Ideation.

Prior to receiving any coaching from me, Jared had naturally applied his Strengths to his professional life and was garnering the benefits that came with flexing his Strengths at work. However, it had not occurred to him that he needed to get gritty with his Strengths at home. Remember, grittiness is a "self-discipline wedded to a dedicated pursuit of a goal."

When Jared recognized that his love for checking things off his to-do list would motivate him get at least two household chores done each day, he found it gratifying to empty the dishwasher every morning. He was half-way done with his household chore goal before 8 AM. Jared's perspective on emptying the dishwasher had shifted. No longer was it a mundane task that took away from the other productive things he wanted to get done. Instead, emptying the dishwasher allowed Jared to tap into both his strategic plan for the week and his love for checking things off his daily to-do list.

Jared's ultimate goal was to have a balanced life. When his home life felt out of balance, he was unable to pour himself into his new business venture. Before having a weekly plan in place that prioritized both home and work tasks, Jared had felt guilty for shirking his responsibilities at home. He was stuck in the same pattern of putting chores off until the weekend and then wasting his cherished unstructured time on Saturday and Sunday playing catch-up.

Harnessing Jared's Strengths more fully allowed him to achieve a more balanced home life and increase his productivity at work. An unforeseen epiphany that came out of his weekly checklists was Jared's new awareness that he could bite off small chunks of enormous work projects in much the same way as he bit off small household chores every day.

In the past, these larger work projects made Jared feel overwhelmed. His old technique for accomplishing these big jobs was to try to carve out at least four hours of time to work on the challenging project to make certain that this time was free from distraction. Jared's new routine of making a weekly strategy and checklist prompted him to see how he could break a huge project into bite-sized pieces and complete a small piece of the larger whole over several days' time. Finding a four-hour block of time was nearly impossible in Jared's busy life. The bite-sized accomplishments allowed Jared to stay on track with his goals.

This new method of tapping into his Strategic and Achiever strengths helped him become gritty. More importantly, becoming gritty helped Jared to become unstuck from his unproductive pattern of putting off chores at home and big projects at work. Utilizing his Strengths where they had not been previously applied, liberated him from chore-filled weekends at home and overwhelming projects at work.

Exercise: Gritty Insights

1. Take Duckworth's assessment of grit:
   www.unstuckatlast.com/resources

   What was your score? Do you think it is accurate?

2. Answer the following questions about grit:

   - Have you ever had a goal that took you years to complete?

   - What kept you on track and committed to completing your goal?

   - How do you react to setbacks?

   - Can you recollect a setback you have had in the last year?

   - How did you respond to it?

3. List two goals that are relevant to you right now. Next to each goal, write out and then repeat out loud a two-sentence gritty attitude that can be used as a mantra to make that goal a reality.

4. Choose two of your Strengths that you have been trying to flex more intentionally to become unstuck. How have you applied your Strengths recently and what kind of positive results have you seen? How might you apply these same Strengths in another area of your life?

ten

Amelioration Means Continual Improvement

The term *amelioration* is rarely used and therefore unknown to many. In my work as a Strengths coach who helps people go from good to great, the idea of amelioration – getting better and better – is a fundamental concept, one that I consider frequently. It also happens that I have a sister, Amy, whose given name is Amelia. For that reason, I have always known the definition of the verb "ameliorate," since our parents frequently reminded us of the meaning behind Amy's name: to make better.

The goal of this book has been to pry you loose and set you free to pursue your greatest dreams, whatever they may be. It is hard to believe that the tools you needed all along have been there, waiting patiently inside you, hoping you would recognize them. I hope this book has shown you that your unique and special qualities, the things that make you you, have been hiding in clear sight.

At this stage, my expectation is that you are feeling less stuck but not quite where you want to be. You should feel like a beautiful work in progress. Maybe you are a piece of art with a lot of potential that has some finishing touches in the works. Possibly you see yourself as a symphony that has been three-quarters of the way completed by its composer. It really doesn't matter which metaphor you choose. What matters is that you see progress and keep plugging along in the same direction. You need to celebrate the small wins that occur when you keep your Strengths, motivators, values, and vision in the forefront of your mind.

Ameliorate at Any Age

This book was not written with a particular age group or gender in mind, because everyone becomes stuck at some point and needs a shove in the right direction. My hope is that everyone who reads it, regardless of demographics, sees their potential to get better, improve, elevate themselves, and change. In other words, my wish is that you are able to become more of who you really are.

My favorite national and international news highlight from 2013 was the remarkable swim of 64-year old Diana Nyad. Nyad was the first person ever to swim from Havana, Cuba, to Florida. Completed on September 2, 2013, it was a treacherous swim accomplished without the aid of a shark cage – a device that protects the swimmer from sharks and has the added benefit of creating a draft that pulls the swimmer along. As Nyad emerged from the ocean, she shared three pieces of advice to the throngs who gathered to cheer her on and the media cameras that hoped to capture this record-setting event.[1]

She had been swimming for 52 hours and therefore her words fresh out of the water both imparted and transcended her obvious exhaustion. Nyad said, "One is we should never, ever give up. Two is you are never too old to chase your dreams. Three is it looks like a solitary sport, but it's a team."

Nyad knows that grit is a key to success. Although she was advised by some to give up her goal, she persisted in following her dream. Nyad's 2013 achievement was her fifth attempt to complete the 110-mile swim. She also knows that age should not limit your dreams. Four of her five attempts occurred when Nyad was at least 60-years old. Finally, Nyad recognized that she could not succeed without champions – people who believed in her Strengths, unconditionally supported her, and helped her to achieve her goals.

In a CNN report of Nyad's historical accomplishment, Nyad was quoted as hoping her swim would inspire Americans who she feared "have gotten depressed, pinned in, pinned down with living lives they don't want." Possibly Nyad thinks Americans are stuck and unsure of how to break free.

Continual Improvement Is Not a New Idea

When I started working full-time in a human resources position in 1991, I quickly realized that organizations worldwide were beginning to adopt practices geared toward continual improvement. W. Edwards Deming had started a revolutionary process geared to perfecting the manufacturing process. Although Deming died in 1993, his long-term impact would live on in organizations around the globe. Continual improvement processes groups cropped up in organizations worldwide. These groups had a similar end-result goal: improve the efficiency, effectiveness, and flexibility of the services delivered.

In much the same way, I challenge you to start a personalized continual improvement process. Age, gender, or success-to-date don't matter. In fact, when the goal is improvement, those who have lacked success in the past may quickly benefit from harnessing their Strengths.

Trying to make each day slightly better, every interaction with others more meaningful, or daily "to-do" list goals more attainable are simple examples of how amelioration can be achieved by those who put their Strengths to use.

This book would not be complete without a final example – a story that exemplifies someone who has used his talents to pursue his dreams. And, remarkably, this individual sits in precisely the same spot you find yourself in now – nervous anticipation.

Matthew claims he was stuck for 25-years. Although Matthew felt the pain of being stuck sharply, it was indiscernible to his friends, neighbors, and colleagues. From afar all seemed well. Post-college Matthew constructed an exciting life for himself living in New York City, working for well-known companies, dating beautiful women, and traveling to far-flung destinations. But over the years, the list of companies he worked for and women he dated seemed to increase. He could not find a company or a partner that he appreciated or appreciated him for the long haul.

Until, at the age of 40, Matthew met and married a drop dead gorgeous and intelligent women he had met on one of his international jaunts. Soon they had a baby girl, and Matthew realized that while he was unstuck personally, his professional life was as terrible as ever. He had either left or been displaced from six jobs over the previous six years. Of course, it did not help that his expertise lay in the financial arena and our nation had been suffering from a serious financial crisis during this same time period.

Matthew came to coaching when he was at the end of his rope. He had moved his family to a mid-sized Southern town when he was given an opportunity at an outplacement organization that went into bankruptcy soon after he joined them. Although he was able to find a new position in short order without moving his family, he knew he was not valued at his new job. As Matthew suspected, a few weeks after contacting me to inquire about coaching, he was once again looking for a new job.

He was filled with wonder that his career had amounted to so little. At the same time, and not surprisingly, Matthew was dismayed that he had not constructed the career he had always imagined. He longed for a fulfilling job and success at work.

Matthew took the Clifton StrengthsFinder® assessment soon after our coaching calls started. He was neither surprised by his Strengths, nor at a loss for words to describe how they had positively impacted him professionally in the past. While our coaching calls did not cause a revolutionary change in his self-understanding, they did provide some fine brushstrokes and ultimately allowed him to use his Strengths more productively as he searched for new leads.

Matthew immediately applied his Strengths of Strategic, Input, and Ideation to facilitate his job search. He constructed a plan to connect with as many hiring organizations as possible (Strategic) by researching the top organizations in his new city (Input). We discussed how his Ideation skills could be used in a variety of positions. Matthew loved being given complex issues, contemplating them, and simplifying them. By combining his Strategic, Input and Ideation skills, Matthew soon had a list of possible leads and, soon after, interviews scheduled.

To succeed in an interview, Matthew would need to fully and deftly apply his Woo and Responsibility talents to win over the interviewer and convince him of his ability to get the job done. He needed to showcase his talents by, first, making a connection with the interviewer and, second, emphasizing his dependability.

The weeks of looking for a new position turned into months. When Matthew and I connected for coaching calls during this difficult period, I reiterated my belief in him and his ability to showcase his talents. He needed this bolstering, and "keep being you and keep using your Strengths" was the mantra I gave him. He was on a mission to find an organization that would appreciate him for what he had to give, not focus on what he lacked. In his past jobs, Matthew's superiors seemed to see his greatest assets as his detriments. His goal was to flip that paradigm and find an organization that valued his natural talents.

Through a lead that came from a friend of a friend, Matthew connected with the president of an organization that temporarily placed information technology specialists from abroad with U.S.-based companies that needed their skills. Their first meeting lasted three hours and was as much a personal conversation as it was an interview. Matthew was able to take his game face off and let his guard down. Matthew had a last found someone he could connect with and who might become his champion. Three weeks after that first meeting, Matthew started working for the president's organization. Within two months, Matthew was traveling internationally on the organization's behalf, wooing potential candidates to join their ranks of information technology specialists.

I was able to talk to Matthew in the middle of this two-week trip to five European cities. It was 1:00 AM his time, but he was excited to fill me in on the details of his new job despite his fatigue. He reported catching himself using his Strengths in his new position every day. Although securing a job and using his Strengths daily brought him great relief, he reported feeling vulnerable in a new way. In the past, his vulnerability stemmed from being misunderstood and underappreciated. In his current situation, he felt more fully acknowledged for his talents and appreciated for what he added to his team, but he was aware of the challenges ahead of him. These challenges – learning a new business and proving his worth every day – were his new vulnerable spots.

Matthew admitted to having a nervous anticipation about the road in front of him. He was at a crucial spot on his Strengths journey, one that signified to me that he was exactly where he needed to be. On a path of continual improvement, Matthew was using his Strengths to grow, ameliorate, and get better at his new job.

He was not yet totally comfortable and relaxed in his new position – and that is completely as it should be. When we grow we should feel safe, but not totally comfortable. Much like the growing pains you had in the middle of the night as a child signaled the fact that your legs were getting longer, the nervous anticipation that Matthew was experiencing was a sign to me that he was in exactly the right spot. He was pushing himself forward in a manner that resembled how he became unstuck. The pivotal difference was that now, instead of feeling the dread, he experienced excitement as he pushed himself into his exciting future.

Henry David Thoreau said,

> *"What you get from achieving your goals is not as important as what you become by achieving your goals."*

I look forward to learning about the nervous anticipation you might be experiencing and the exciting future in front of you. Tapping into the real you every day fortifies you – it gives you strength and resiliency in good times and in bad.

Becoming unstuck is a reward in itself because of who you are able to become and what you are able to accomplish. Continue to press forward and know that I am a champion in your corner, cheering you on every step of the way.

Notes & Citations

Chapter One

1. Cameron, J. (1992). *The artist's way: A spiritual path to higher creativity.* Los Angeles, CA: Jeremy P. Tarcher/Perigee.

   To anyone who has artistic aspirations, I highly recommend reading Cameron's classic book. I've read it twice and enjoyed it immensely both times.

2. Dweck, C. (2006). *Mindset: The new psychology of success.* New York: Random House.

3. Stella Terrill Mann Quotes. (n.d.). *Quotes.net.* Retrieved February 1, 2015, from http://www.quotes.net/quote/15413.

Chapter Two

1. Rath, T. (2007). *StrengthsFinder 2.0.* New York, NY: Gallup Press.

2. ChaWare, B. (2012). *The top five regrets of the dying: A life transformed by the dearly departing.* Carlsbad, Calif.: Hay House.

3. I wrote a blog that explored how inauthentic living brings regret and stumbled upon this book. The insights of the author stuck with me.

4. Sandberg, S., & Scovell, N. (n.d.). *Lean in: Women, work, and the will to lead.*

    Sandberg, Facebook's COO, is a huge fan of Strengths – in fact, Facebook employees are asked to take the StrengthsFinder® assessment. Her book on women and leadership reminded me of all the lessons I learned at Mount Holyoke College about power, feminism, and the importance of being outspoken.

Chapter Three

1. Sandberg, S., & Scovell, N. (n.d.). Lean in: Women, work, and the will to lead.

Chapter Five

1. Heath, C., & Heath, D. (2007). Made to stick: Why some ideas survive and others die. New York: Random House.

    All of Dan and Chip Heath's books (check out *Switch and Decisive*) are thought-provoking and fun to read. Why stop here?

Chapter Six

1. DuBrin, A. (2007). *Fundamentals of organizational behavior* (4th ed.). Mason, OH: Thomson/South-Western.

    Andrew DuBrin and I do not know one another, but he feels like a friend. This is the textbook I have used for over a decade. I think of it as an organizational behavior bible.

Chapter Seven

1. Shellenbarger, S. (n.d.). WSJ Blogs - WSJ. Retrieved February 1, 2015, from http://blogs.wsj.com/

   Shellenbarger writes the "Family & Work" column for the WSJ Blog.

2. Greenleaf, R., & Frick, D. (1996). *On becoming a servant-leader.* San Francisco: Jossey-Bass.

3. Spears, L. (1995). *Reflections on leadership: How Robert K. Greenleaf's theory of Servant-leadership influenced today's top management thinkers.* New York: J. Wiley.

   I ask my students to read an excerpt from the Spears reading to gain an overview of Greenleaf's understanding of servant leadership.

4. Achor, S. (2010). *The happiness advantage: The seven principles of positive psychology that fuel success and performance at work.* New York: Broadway Books.

   Shaun Achor is a great author who is able to dole out many practical tips on becoming happier while sharing important research on the subject.

5. http://www.inc.com/jessica-stillman/youre-praising-your-employees-the-wrong-way.html

   I mention the importance of praising the effort and not the result of children, but the same goes for employees. This article found on the Inc. website does a good job summarizing the issue.

Chapter Eight

1. If somehow you're not acquainted with "The Office", take a few moments to watch Michael Scott and his

enormous ego in action.
http://www.tbs.com/shows/the-office.html

Chapter Nine

1. Tough, P. (n.d.). How children succeed: Grit, curiosity, and the hidden power of character.

2. Duckworth, A., & Quinn, P. (n.d.). Development and Validation Of The Short Grit Scale (Grit-S). Journal of Personality Assessment, 166-174.

3. Rudy [Motion picture]. (1993). Tri Star Pictures.

4. Phillips, D. (1992). Lincoln on leadership: Executive strategies for tough times. New York: Warner Books.

   Phillips's book on Lincoln is a quick read and has great tips for managers.

Chapter Ten

1. Press, A. (2013, September 2). Diana Nyad completes Cuba-Florida swim. Retrieved February 2, 2015, from http://www.usatoday.com/story/sports/2013/09/02/di ana-nyad-cuba-florida-swim/2754645/

2. Deming, W. (1986). *Out of the crisis*. Cambridge, Mass.: Massachusetts Institute of Technology, Center for Advanced Engineering Study.

Unstuck At Last

My Top 5 Strengths

1. _____

2. _____

3. _____

4. _____

5. _____

My Top 5 Motivators

1. _____

2. _____

3. _____

4. _____

5. _____

My Top 2 Values

1. _____

2. _____

My Vision Image

Acknowledgments

I am so grateful to Nicole Gebhardt, of TheRemarkable-Way.com, for her guidance, wisdom, kindness, and unflappable encouragement. Special thanks to Madelaine Cooke for donating her remarkable skills and making me believe this might really be a book. To Lori Cranford, at Rare Bird, who helped me immensely when I was literally at my wits' end. And thanks to Jim Cota, my go-to guy at Rare Bird, for his artistic eye and strategic mind.

To my first, middle, and last reader, David, no words can express my gratitude to and for you. Eternal thanks and love to my small band of champions Lisa, Char, Dana, Anne-Marie, Krista, Amy, Elizabeth, Rene, Lee, Andrea, Brigid, and Cheryl.

About the Author

Sarah Robinson is a business owner, Gallup Certified Strengths Coach, Associate Faculty member, and community volunteer. For more than 20 years, she has performed organizational development training for a variety of companies in the for-profit and non-profit fields. In 2013, Sarah became the first of seven consultants worldwide to be certified by Gallup as an Individual and Team Coach using the Clifton StrengthsFinder® assessment. Coupling her organizational behavior expertise with her skills as a StrengthsFinder® coach, Sarah helps her clients more fully maximize their potential – professionally and personally.

Sarah's "Top 5 Signature Themes" are Competition, Maximizer, Achiever, Activator, and Significance. In simple language, this means she works to obtain measureable outcomes for her clients – results that lift them from good to great. Sarah greatly enjoys helping her clients create new plans that can immediately be put into action. Ultimately, coaching allows Sarah to leverage her signature themes and her professional abilities to improve the lives of her clients.

Sarah received her Master's in Industrial and Organizational Psychology in 1991. In 1992, she received her designation as a Professional in Human Resources (PHR) from the Society of Human Resources Management (SHRM). She has taught the course "Managing Behavior for Public Organizations" for the School of Public and Environmental Affairs at I.U.P.U.I. since 2002.

Sarah is known for her enthusiasm – in the classroom, as a presenter, and as a Strengths Coach. She enjoys meeting her clients' needs while challenging herself to learn more about the ever-growing discipline of organizational behavior. Sarah lives with her family and ill-behave chocolate Labrador Retriever in Indianapolis, Indiana.

Contact Sarah at **www.unstuckatlast.com** to obtain more information about her speaking schedule, upcoming workshops, as well as individual and corporate coaching.

Made in the USA
San Bernardino, CA
08 December 2015